EXCELLENT
SHORT
WALKS

IN THE SOUTH ISLAND

EXCELLENT SHORT WALKS

IN THE SOUTH ISLAND

OVER 250 WALKS UNDER 2 HOURS

PETER JANSSEN

NEW
HOLLAND

To Peter R. who always tells it straight and always
makes me laugh.

First published in 2008 by New Holland Publishers (NZ) Ltd
Auckland • Sydney • London • Cape Town

www.newhollandpublishers.co.nz

218 Lake Road, Northcote, Auckland 0627, New Zealand
Unit 1, 66 Gibbes Street, Chatswood, NSW 2067, Australia
86–88 Edgware Road, London W2 2EA, United Kingdom
80 McKenzie Street, Cape Town 8001, South Africa

ISBN: 978 1 86966 190 8

Publishing manager: Christine Thomson
Editor: Mike Wagg
Design team: IslandBridge, Justine Mackenzie
Cover design: Trevor Newman
Front cover photograph: Upper Waimakariri River (Hedgehog House/Colin Monteath)
Maps: Bruce McLennan/IslandBridge

National Library of New Zealand Cataloguing-in-Publication Data
    Janssen, Peter (Peter Leon)
    Excellent short walks in the South Island / text and photography
    by Peter Janssen ; edited by Mike Wagg.
    ISBN 978-1-86966-190-8
    1. Trails—New Zealand—South Island—Guidebooks.
    2. South Island (N.Z)—Description and travel. I. Wagg, Mike.
    II. Title.
    796.5109937—dc 22

10 9 8 7 6 5 4 3

Colour reproduction by Pica Digital Pte Ltd, Singapore
Printed by Times Offset (M) Sdn Bhd, Malaysia, on paper sourced from sustainable forests.

Contents

Buller   44

South Canterbury, Mackenzie Country and Mt Cook   95

North and East Otago   105

South Otago and the Catlins

Introduction

For many years I've been a keen walker throughout New Zealand, but I often find that the longer trips, while enjoyable, are a bit much to tackle; for example, when I'm travelling or when I don't have the necessary gear to hand. And on many occasions I have visitors who are keen to 'get out and about' but do not have the time, experience or equipment for longer trips.

I have discovered, however, that there are many excellent short walks to be found throughout the country, and that you don't have to tramp for hours to savour some of the best scenery or experiences New Zealand has to offer. Like its companion volume, *Excellent Short Walks in the North Island*, this book is a collection of what I think are excellent short walks and encompass bush, coastal, urban, mountain and alpine country. Each walk has a highlight (or several highlights) so you can pick and choose to suit your tastes and time. No special gear is necessary, the walks are not hard to find, and you won't get lost. You will not need to take food or water, though in summer on some of the longer walks water will be appreciated, and an energy bar or two never goes amiss.

While many areas of the South Island are remote and mountainous, it is possible to access spectacular alpine scenery from the mountain passes, walk through virgin rainforest, stroll alone along a remote beach and see rare animals up close.

So whether you are eight years old or eighty, these walks should suit almost everyone. Now all you have to do is stop the car, get out and get walking!

How to use this book

It is worth pointing out that *Excellent Short Walks in the South Island* is intended to be a fund of ideas rather than a blow-by-blow track guide. The brevity of the walks removes the need for detailed track notes, and any walks that were hard to follow have not been included. Some authorities are great with signage, others are hopeless, while some don't take into account visitors and just assume that walkers are local and know where to go. However, I have been reluctant to be too critical regarding poor signage as it is often destroyed or vandalised, rather than not existing in the first place.

Point of interest ✳

Each walk has as its destination a point of interest. In some cases this will be a true ruby in the dust – a hidden gem among otherwise unremarkable surroundings – while in others, particularly the more remote and scenic spots, you will be spoilt for choice.

How to get there ➤

These descriptions assume that the traveller has a reasonable road atlas and, in urban areas, a street map. The excellent network of information centres and Department of Conservation offices will be able to help out if you don't have a local map or are really unsure of directions.

Grade ⅄

Easy   Can be managed by almost everyone; mainly flat to rolling, and generally in good condition. However, these walks can include steps, short steep sections, a bit of mud and the occasional rough patch.

Medium Will include rough stretches, muddy patches and steps or steep sections.

Hard   In short this really means steep. These walks will require a bit of fitness and a little uphill sweat.

Time

The times given are conservative and assume a very leisurely pace. A fit person can expect to take 25 to 30 per cent less time than stated.

The times given on information boards also tend to be very conservative. Don't be put off by what seems a long walk – they are usually much shorter.

Gear

No special gear is required for these walks, but New Zealand weather is notoriously fickle and the conditions of the tracks vary considerably, so be prepared. The weather in the South Island can turn cold quickly, even in summer, and the West Coast of the South Island is famous for its high rainfall. Thermal underclothing is a good warm option and very light to wear.

Shoes: Tramping boots are not necessary. You will be much more comfortable with a good pair of trainers that you don't mind getting dirty and which have good tread. Tracks are often muddy or have slippery sections over rocks and wooden steps.

Jacket: Invest in a jacket that is rain-proof. Many jackets are only shower- or wind-proof and it rains a lot in New Zealand. If you don't want to go to the expense, then those heavy yellow plastic coats may not be elegant bushwear, but they are cheap and certainly keep the rain out. In wetter seasons, keeping a few dry clothes in the car is a good idea so that if you do get wet you have something warm to change into.

A word about jandals

Jandals are about as Kiwi as it gets, but they are absolutely hopeless on walking tracks. Once wet you will slip out of them easily, and in the wet they flick mud up the back of your legs. Even worse, you are likely to snap the thong and break your very best jandals, which is very distressing. Just don't wear them when walking. If you don't like shoes, there are now plenty of sturdy sandals that have decent tread and offer good support.

Security

An unfortunate fact of life in modern New Zealand is that car burglary is now common in walk car parks. Some very popular attractions now even have security guards. Short of leaving someone with the car at all times, there are a few things you can do to lessen the chances of having your car broken into. Lock your car even on the short walks, and double-check your windows are closed (it is easy to forget your back windows). Make sure that all valuables are out of sight, and if possible carry your most valuable items with you (wallet, camera, phone, video). Invest in an inexpensive steering lock: this won't stop your car being broken into, but it will indicate to thieves that you are security-conscious and it will almost certainly stop them actually stealing the car.

Mobile phones

Mobile phones can be very useful if you are lost, but be aware they do not always have coverage in some of the more remote places.

Sandflies

New Zealand may not have snakes or dangerous animals, but sandflies can make that walk in the bush or picnic hell. Small and black, the sandfly packs a nasty bite, which then leaves you scratching for some time afterwards. Only the female bites, requiring blood to produce her eggs, and since she lays these in water, it follows that sandflies are particularly prolific in the wetter bush areas. They are a real nuisance along the entire West Coast and the wetter northern areas.

The good news is that sandflies are easily deterred by insect repellent, which is readily available in supermarkets and chemists in roll-on or spray-on form. A citronella-based natural insect repellent called *Bite Back* is also available.

Giardia

Giardia is an invisible water-borne parasite now common in New Zealand streams, and if ingested it can ruin your holiday. The symptoms are diarrhoea, a bloated feeling in your stomach and a loss of appetite. No matter how clean or pure the water looks, it can still contain giardia and you should always boil or filter water before drinking it.

Acknowledgements

Many thanks to all the folks at information centres and DoC offices who have not only been very helpful but also enthusiastic and supportive. A special thanks to Mike Wagg for all his polite patience in editing the book, and the staff at New Holland, who have backed this project from the beginning.

Marlborough

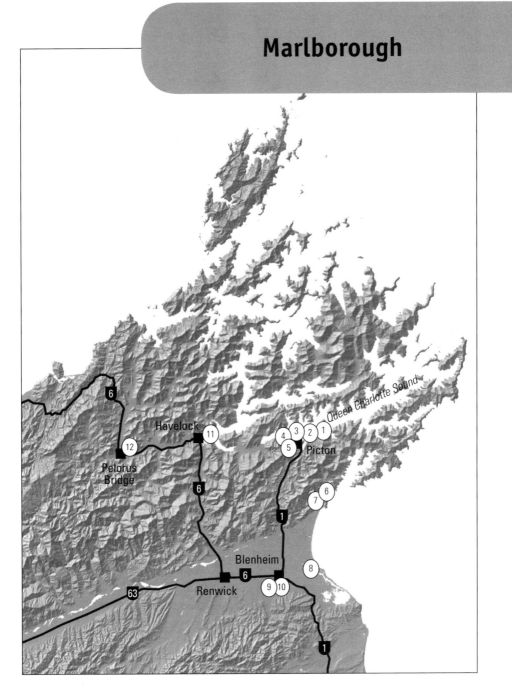

Picton

1 Karaka Point Track   Easy   🚶   20 minutes return

✳ Great views combined with a well-preserved historic pa site.

➤ From Picton, take the Waikawa Road to Waikawa Bay and then continue along the narrow road towards Port Underwood. The walk is well marked on the left-hand side of the road.

Te Pae o Te Karaka pa was named after the Ngati Mamoe chief Te Karaka who settled here in the early 1700s. Later taken by Ngai Tahu, the pa was attacked and captured in the 1820s by musket-wielding Te Atiawa and subsequently abandoned and never reoccupied. As well as great views over Queen Charlotte Sound, this pa is well preserved, with the clear outlines of defensive ditches, house sites and kumara pits. Tracks lead down to two shingle beaches.

2 Queen Charlotte View/The Snout   Medium

✳ Scenic ridge along a narrow peninsula jutting far out into the sound.

➤ From Picton, take the Waikawa Road, then turn left into Loop Drive, which is clearly marked and is one-way. Continue along the drive to the car park just before the road turns sharply downhill to the right. The track begins from the northern side of this car park.

🚶 To Queen Charlotte View: 1 hour 20 minutes return

To The Snout: 2½ hours return

After a 10-minute walk along a wide access road flanked by gorse, the track then narrows and enters regenerating native bush with expansive views that unfurl the further along the peninsula you go. Queen Charlotte Sound is often busy with small pleasure boats, and if you time it right a Cook Strait ferry may well glide past below.

From Queen Charlotte View there are excellent outlooks far to the north, while on both sides of the peninsula numerous bays and bush-clad ridges line the sound leading back to the town of Picton behind you.

The end of the peninsula, known as The Snout, is a further 35 minutes from Queen Charlotte View. Interestingly, this promontory's expressive Maori name, Te Ihumoeone-ihu, translates as 'the nose of the sand worm'.

3 Bob's Bay   Easy   ⅄   1 hour return

✳ Attractive bay with a grassy picnic area within easy walk of Picton town.

➤ Cross over the footbridge north of the town centre and walk along the shoreline past the marina to where the beginning of the walk is marked. (If you drive to the track, watch where you park as certain areas are reserved for boat owners only.)

A popular walk and easy to undertake from town, the Lower Bob's Bay Track closely follows the coastline through regenerating bush to Bob's Bay. With clear water ideal for swimming, the beach is a mixture of sand and gravel, while a large and attractive grassy picnic area with toilet facilities is located behind.

Return the same way, but this time turn left at the second 'Harbour View Terrace' sign, which leads to the higher track, also referred to as the Upper Bob's Bay Track. When the marina comes into view, take the right-hand track back down to the water's edge where you started.

4 Tirohanga Walkway/Hilltop View   Medium

✳ Excellent views over Picton and Queen Charlotte Sound.

➤ From the south end of Nelson Square in Picton, go up Devon Street to Garden Terrace. Park on the road, cross the ford, and the track starts on your left.

⅄ 1¼ hours return
   If walking up from the town: add 30 minutes

This is a great walk to obtain an overview of the complex nature of Queen Charlotte Sound, with its numerous bays, inlets and islands, from the lookout point at the top of the hill. Although it is a steady to steep climb through regenerating bush to the lookout, the track is in good condition and you are more than likely to have the company of friendly fantails along the way. If you have the time, you can continue on down the loop track back to Picton, where it emerges on Newgate Street to the east of the town centre.

5 Humphries Dam Easy 🚶 1 hour 20 minutes return

✳ A deep valley with mature trees, site of one of Picton's water reservoirs.

➤ From the south end of Picton's Nelson Square, go down Devon Street to Garden Terrace where the track starts to the right at the end.

The first section of the track starts out rather unpromisingly and follows a 4WD road through regenerating bush in a broad valley. However, it soon narrows, as does the valley, and the bush here is in direct contrast to the more scrubby vegetation more characteristic of the Marlborough Sounds. Mature beech trees dominate, with an occasional large tawa and rimu, while the forest floor is lush with mosses and ferns flourishing in the deep, damp, cool shade.

The track meanders along a clear and rocky stream following the town water supply pipeline to a small concrete dam deep in bush and perfect for a swim on a hot day. If you are interested in extending the walk, a side track leads off to another reservoir, Barnes Dam. There is also a large grass picnic area and a good swimming hole just 200 metres from the car park at the beginning of the track.

Blenheim

6 Whites Bay

✳ Secluded, bush-lined bay with historic Maori and European features.

➤ From Blenheim, take the road to Rarangi Beach and Port Underwood. Where the road starts climbing uphill at Rarangi, drive a further 4 km to Whites Bay.

The coast of Cloudy Bay is not known for its beaches, but tucked away on the road to Port Underwood are a number of very pretty bays including Whites Bay, named after an African-American slave, Black Jack White, who jumped ship in 1828 in Port Underwood and then settled in the area. Pukatea Pa is located on the bay's south-west corner and the Treaty of Waitangi was signed just to the north on Horahora Kakahu Island. The first Cook Strait telegraph cable was hauled ashore here in 1886, linking the South Island to Lyall Bay in Wellington, and the telegraph building, which was prefabricated in Australia and housed staff from 1867 to 1873, is still on site today.

Three short walks lead up from the small, sandy, bush-clad bay, which is in direct contrast to the dry open country south of the Wairau River. The tracks begin from the information board to the left of the historic cable station, and there is a good camping site and safe swimming here.

Black Jack Loop/Port Underwood Lookout   Medium

🚶 Black Jack Loop: 1¼ hours

Port Underwood Lookout: 1 hour return

The Black Jack Loop and Port Underwood Lookout track is in excellent condition and is a steady rather than steep uphill climb through bush, with the occasional glimpse through the trees over Cloudy Bay. The track then follows a ridge to the lookout over Port Underwood and Cook Strait. The return leg of the loop begins about 100 metres past the lookout point and is downhill all the way back to Whites Bay.

Pukatea Loop   Easy   🚶   25 minutes return

This short walk can be added to the end of the above walks, and follows a stream through the bush that eventually emerges on the road to Whites Bay. While the bush is not anything special, you are more likely to see native birds, such as fantail, kereru, tui and bellbird, in this area.

7 Monkey Bay   Easy   🚶   15 minutes return

✳ A pretty shingle cove, dramatic in a southerly swell.

➤ From Blenheim, take the road to Rarangi Beach and Port Underwood. At the north end of Rarangi Beach, just before the road starts to climb the hill, turn right to the beginning of the track.

This brief walk climbs a short flight of beautifully built stone steps over a small bluff to a little shingle cove open to the southerly swells, and giving excellent views south over Cloudy Bay and Cape Campbell. A sea arch pierces the rock behind the bay, which booms in heavy weather as the waves crash into the small opening. Local legend has it that the name comes from an escaped monkey that made the bay its home. You can walk to Whites Bay from here, but you will need to return the same way unless you have arranged transport to pick you up.

8 Wairau Lagoon   Easy   🚶   Allow up to 2 hours

* ✳ Ecologically significant wetland along Wairau River estuary and the shores of Cloudy Bay.

* ➤ End of Hardings Road, 5.5 km south of Blenheim off SH1.

Although this walk begins through the middle of Blenheim's sewerage treatment plant, it quickly emerges onto a vast salt marsh of interlacing waterways that is home to some unique salt-tolerant plants and is alive with aquatic bird life. The track meanders through this area, and while generally well maintained, is quite wet and boggy in places. A special feature is the wreck of the steamer *Waverley*. Built in New Zealand in 1883, the 125-ton ship was dismantled in Wellington in 1928 and then sunk at the mouth of the Wairau River to act as a breakwater.

The Wairau Bar was the main port for Blenheim until an earthquake in 1855 dropped the level of the entire Wairau Plain, deepening the Opawa River in the process and allowing shipping access further inland. It is also one of New Zealand's most important archaeological sites. Moa-hunter Maori used the bar as a base, and evidence suggests that they slaughtered over 8000 of these giant birds and consumed over 2000 moa eggs.

9 Rotary Lookout/Quails Junction   Medium

* ✳ Extensive views over the Wairau Plains, Richmond Range and Cook Strait.

* ➤ From Blenheim, take Maxwell Road and continue on Taylor Pass Road. The beginning of the track is on your left from the well-signposted car park.

* 🚶 Rotary Lookout: 45 minutes return
  Quails Junction: 1½ hours return

The strikingly beautiful and bare Wither Hills form a dramatic backdrop to the burgeoning town of Blenheim, and a great appeal of walking here is that the views are constant and forever unfolding. Numerous tracks and access points provide walks of every type, though for most visitors the Taylor Pass Road entrance is the most popular and accessible.

From the car park, the Gentle Annie Track to the left of the information board winds up through a gully to the Rotary Lookout, which has both seating and a shelter. The hills, tawny brown in summer, provide an impressive backdrop to views over Blenheim and the vine-covered Wairau Plains below. To the north-west is the rugged Richmond Range, while to the east is Cloudy Bay, the wild Cook Strait, and the North Island visible beyond.

If you are feeling fit, continue uphill to Quails Junction on the Twin Tracks Walk to even more impressive views, and then return down the Lower Quail Stream Walk. This walk is especially attractive in the mellow light of the morning and evening.

10 Sutherland Stream/Mt Vernon Lookout

✸ Excellent views over Blenheim, the Wairau Plains, Cloudy Bay and Cook Strait.

➤ The tracks begin at the car park at the southern end of Redwood Street, Blenheim.

🚶 Sutherland Stream: Easy, 1 hour return

Mt Vernon Lookout: Medium, 2 hours return

The sparse grass and tussock of the Wither Hills is now such an integral part of Marlborough that it is difficult to believe this terrain was once covered in dense native forest. Maori destroyed much of the initial forest by fire, either deliberately or accidentally, and what little was left was cleared by early European settlers. Once gone, the bush never recovered, and a recent fire in 2000 (very evident on this walk) demonstrates the fragile nature of this landscape in a climate of dry summers with strong warm winds.

The easy walk to the picnic area along Sutherland Stream is one of the few flat walks within the Wither Hills Farm Park and follows a swampy stream, passing through replanting of vegetation native to this area.

The Mt Vernon Lookout is a 2-hour loop walk beginning at the same car park. First take the Ridgeline Track (this has the easier uphill grade), and, as the name suggests, follows the ridgeline. Proceed through the tawny open tussock country to a wonderful lookout point with the town spread below and views far out over Cloudy Bay and Cook Strait. Return down the Covenant Track to the Sutherland Stream Track and back to the car park.

Marlborough

11 Cullen's Point Lookout/Mahaki Paoa
Easy 𝕏 20 minutes return

✴ An easy walk to a viewpoint over the Mahau Sound.

➤ Queen Charlotte Drive, 3 km from Havelock.

This short walk through bush (with some steps) leads to a lookout point high above Mahau Sound with views along the sound and beyond to the town of Havelock, famous for its mussels farmed in the rich waters of the Sounds.

12 Pelorus Bridge

✴ Magnificent untouched forest along the banks of the picturesque Pelorus and Rai rivers.

➤ SH6, 18 km west of Havelock.

Several short bush walks around the Pelorus Bridge at the junction of the Pelorus and Rai rivers give access to some of the best mature lowland forest in the Marlborough region. In addition to black, red, hard and silver beech there are miro, tawa, totara and kahikatea, and some of these trees, such as miro, are not found further south. Bird life includes bellbirds, tui, kereru and kakariki, as well as the occasional kaka. A bridge was first built here in 1859, although prior to that an old Maori trail through this area linked Tasman Bay to the Sounds. It was also around these parts that the notorious Burgess Gang murdered four local men for their gold, though they were soon captured and brought to justice.

There is an excellent café with homemade food at Pelorus Bridge, and also good spots for swimming in the river. All four walks start from the car park by the café and the Tawa and Totara walks are both dead flat, so even the most walk-averse members of the party shouldn't grumble!

Tawa Walk   Easy 𝕏 25 minutes return

This loop walk ambles through magnificent virgin kahikatea and tawa with a dense understorey of ferns, mosses and shrubs.

Totara Walk   Easy   🚶   25 minutes return

Beginning across the road from the car park, this walk leads through beech and totara, and there is a much more open understorey, with the forest floor in parts a solid carpet of fern. There is one particularly impressive large totara, and two short side tracks lead down to excellent large swimming holes in the river.

Circle Walk   Easy   🚶   30 minutes return

This track begins immediately to the right across the road bridge and is flat to the substantial suspension bridge over the Rai River where it joins the Pelorus. Beyond the bridge, the track then forms a loop, part of which follows the high bank of the Pelorus with views over the water and Totara Flat.

Waterfall Walk   Medium   🚶   2 hours return

This is a well-formed track, if a bit rougher than the shorter tracks, that leads to two small waterfalls on the Pelorus River. Return the same way.

Nelson

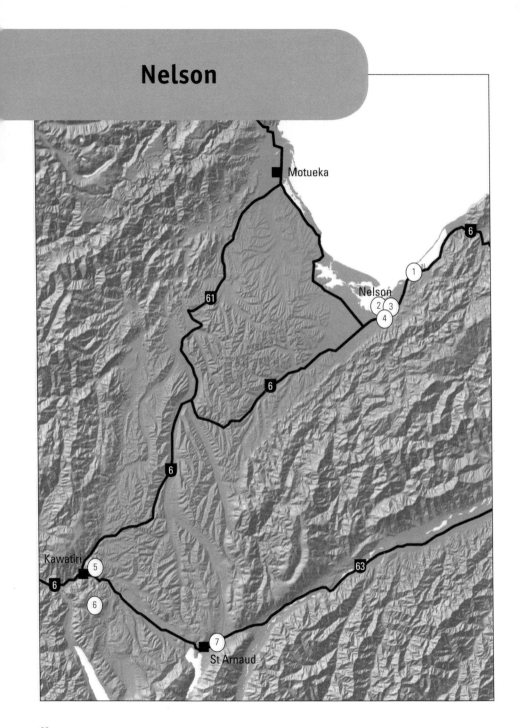

1 Cable Bay

* ✳ Great views west over Tasman Bay and to the mountains beyond.

* ➤ From Nelson, take SH6 towards Picton and after 12 km turn left into Cable Bay Road and continue another 8 km to the beach. The track starts to the left.

* 🚶 To information board lookout: Easy, 5 minutes

  To top of the hill: Hard, 50 minutes return

The shingle beach at Cable Bay was the exit point for the first international telegraph cable from New Zealand to Sydney, laid in 1876. Prior to this, the bay was known by its Maori name, Rotokura. A short climb leads to an excellent information board relating the history of the telegraph cable.

The Cable Bay walkway runs from the left of Cable Bay beach up through farmland, bush remnants and pine forest to the Glen. The entire walk takes 2½ hours one-way. While both ends have short walks to lookouts with great views, the Cable Bay end is the more attractive walk, but a solid uphill slog. Watch out for the electric fence near the top of the hill as it runs very close to the track. The loop walk from the Glen is a more steady uphill, though the track is rough and the landscape less attractive.

There are terrific views over Tasman Bay, the Boulder Bank and the north-west Nelson mountains.

Nelson City

2 Nelson Botanic Reserve/Centre of New Zealand
Medium 🚶 30 minutes return

* ✳ The birthplace of New Zealand rugby and a lookout point over Nelson City.

* ➤ The Botanic Reserve is across the footbridge over the Matai River at the end of Hardy Street, and the track to the Centre of New Zealand begins on the far side of the reserve.

On 14 May 1870 the first game of rugby in New Zealand was played on this field between Nelson Football Club (Town) and Nelson College. The Nelson Football Club originally played an odd mix of soccer and Victorian (Australian) Rules football, but in 1870 changed its name to the Nelson Rugby Club, thereby becoming the first rugby club in the country. At that stage rugby was played between teams of 20 and points could only be scored by kicking goals. However, before a goal could be kicked, the ball had to be first touched down, which then gave that team the right to 'try' for a goal. For the record, Town beat College 2 goals to nil.

The Centre of New Zealand walk begins from the Botanic Reserve and leads up a short but steep hill to a great viewing point over the city and beyond. Contrary to popular local belief, it is not the geographical centre of New Zealand, but a convenient hill used by an early surveyor, John Browning, who was charged by the government to link up earlier surveys. To extend the walk you can return to the city via the Matai Valley.

3 Maitai River Easy ⅄ 1 hour

* ✳ An enjoyable riverside stroll through central Nelson to the Cricket Ground.

* ➤ Begins by the river at the back of the car park behind the information centre, corner of Trafalgar and Halifax Streets.

This pleasant riverside walk begins from the central business area and follows the right-hand bank through the suburbs of Nelson to the Nelson Cricket Ground on the outskirts of the city. Initially the river is tidal, and a worthwhile short side trip not far from the start is the Queens Gardens, an immaculate formal Victorian garden. There are swimming holes along the river, the first just above the Nile Street East Bridge, and two more by the cricket ground including a rope swing at the Black Hole.

From the cricket ground, it is a 35-minute walk back to the start via Matai Road and Nile Street, or you can detour to the right and take in the Centre of New Zealand and the Botanic Reserve (see above) on the way back.

4 The Grampians Medium

* ✳ Superb views over Nelson City and Tasman Bay.

* ➤ The walk begins from the corner of Trafalgar Street South and Van Diemen Street behind the historic Fairfield House.

⅄ Trig: 30 minutes return
Lookout: 1½ hours

Nelson

The Grampians are the hills situated directly south of the city topped by communications towers, and the views from the platform near the summit are reward enough for the uphill trek. While there are several entrances to this area, most are badly marked, so if you are a visitor to Nelson either start at Fairfield House or at the very end of Collingwood Street in the city.

The walk begins with a solid uphill climb on a zigzag path to the trig, which has good views over the city. If you find this section a physical challenge then be aware that there are several more similarly steep climbs to the top lookout, so you might like to just stop here.

The lookout is just to the right of the last uphill section to the transmitter. The views are fantastic, far out over the Waimea Plains, the mountains to the west, Tasman Bay to the north, with the city laid out below. There is no point trudging right up to the transmitter as this is overgrown and there are no views (although the base of the tower does feature some innovative and amusing, if somewhat obscene, graffiti).

5 Kawatiri Railway   Easy   🚶   30 minutes return

✱ A pleasant river and bush walk with an historic railway bridge and tunnel.

➤ The walk begins near the junction of SH6 and SH63.

The Nelson/Inangahua railway was intended to link Nelson to the West Coast and in 1929 reached Gowanbridge, just south of Kawatiri junction. Despite strong public pressure for it to continue, the line was never completed. Its closure in 1955 was accompanied by vigorous protest by local women, who staged a sit-in on the track, and included Sonia Davies who went on to become a well-known trade union activist and Labour Member of Parliament.

From the car park, the track follows the old railway embankment to the remains of a railway bridge over the Hope River, now topped by a footbridge. Over the bridge, the track leads to the Pikomanu Tunnel, with the date of construction – 1923 – proudly proclaimed above the entrance. While a torch is not necessary, it is wet and uneven underfoot. Just beyond the tunnel are the concrete foundations of yet another bridge. The loop walk continues to the left up a short flight of steps through beech forest, passing by a shallow cave that was once the explosives store.

At the car park there are excellent photos and information on the railway line as well as the remains of the original road bridge.

Nelson Lakes

Formed during the last ice age, both Lake Rotoiti and Lake Rotoroa are the result of glacier action in the mountains of the Upper Buller River. Reaching into the heart of the most northern section of the Southern Alps, the lakes give access to both lower forest, mainly consisting of silver and red beech, and true alpine terrain, which is deep in snow in winter. The birdlife in the 102,000-hectare forest is prolific and includes bellbirds, robins and kaka.

The Department of Conservation information centre in St Arnaud at Lake Rotoiti has excellent displays on the natural environment, and up-to-date information on walks in the area. While Lake Rotoroa is larger and deeper, Lake Rotoiti is more accessible and has a wider range of facilities. Water taxis operate on both lakes, which is a convenient way to access more remote parts of their shores, while a lake cruise operates on Lake Rotoiti.

6 Lake Rotoroa   Easy

* ✳ Magnificent beech forest on the edge of Lake Rotoroa.

* ➤ Turn off SH6, 12 km north of Gowanbridge, or 6 km south of Kawatiri junction.

* 🚶 Lake Rotoroa Nature Walk: 25 minutes

  Flowers Brothers Track: 10 minutes return

Both these short walks start from the car park by the boat ramp.

The Nature Walk is a loop track that begins to the left of the car park and continues along the lake edge with views across the water and deep into the mountains. Old kowhai trees overhang the placid water and massive beech trees soar into the sky, while a solid layer of crown ferns carpets the forest floor.

The Flowers Brothers Track goes in the opposite direction and leads through a stand of kahikatea to the outlet of the lake that forms the Gowan River.

7 Lake Rotoiti

✳ A lakeside 'mainland island' for the preservation of native birds.

➤ The walks start from Kerr Bay in the St Arnaud township on SH63 between Blenheim and Murchison.

🚶 Bellbird Walk: Easy, 10 minutes

Honey Dew Walk: Easy, 30 minutes

Loop Walk: Medium, 1½ hours

These three walks begin from the eastern side of Kerr Bay and are essentially loop walks, each progressively longer than the other, so it is very easy to find one here to suit all abilities. The forest is part of a 'mainland island' scheme whereby predators are eradicated and permanently excluded from a section of forest, allowing native birds to recover and flourish. Keep an eye out and you might glimpse two of New Zealand's rarer parrots, the kaka and kakariki.

The Bellbird Walk is an easy walk along the lake and through a short section of forest, while the Honey Dew Walk continues further along the shore and then takes a slight uphill before looping back through bush.

The longest track is the Loop Walk that follows the shoreline past several small beaches and then becomes a steady uphill as it follows a ridge through open beech forest. This track can be rough underfoot and muddy in parts, and the open nature of the forest means you need to check regularly that you are following the orange triangle markers.

Golden Bay

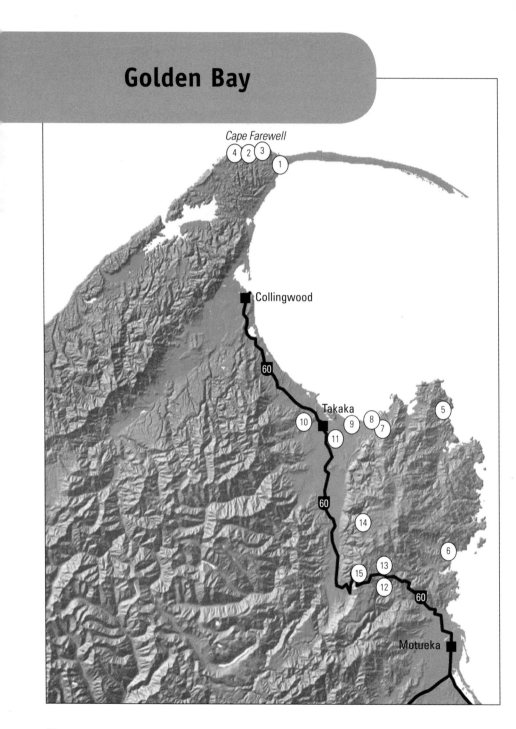

Cape Farewell

4 2 3
1

■ Collingwood

60

Takaka
10 ■
11   9 8 7   5

60

14

13
15 12
60

Motueka ■

Farewell Spit

An irresistible combination of the wild West Coast and the gentle reaches of Golden Bay sheltered by the broad sweep of Farewell Spit, this area has in many ways the best of everything New Zealand has to offer.

Over 30 km in length, Farewell Spit is one of the longest recurved sand spits in the world. The area's delicate ecosystem is home to a rich variety of bird life (over 90 species have been recorded), including migratory birds such as godwits and red knots that arrive in their tens of thousands in the spring and feed in the shallow waters of Golden Bay. However, these shallows are also a death trap for whales and the bay is the site of regular strandings, mainly by pilot whales.

There is an excellent information centre and café with displays on the natural history of the locale (closed June to August), and at the end of the spit are an old lighthouse and gannet colony. In order to preserve the environment, access is limited to two tour operators: Farewell Spit Eco Tours (www.FarewellSpit.com) and Farewell Spit Nature Experience (www.farewell-spit.co.nz).

1 Farewell Spit Beaches   Easy   🏃 1½ hours

* A loop walk that includes both the 'inside' and 'outside' beaches of the spit.

➤ At Puponga, turn right and follow the road to the beach just beyond the information centre, or you can park at the information centre and take the short walk down to the beach.

The walk is located within the Puponga Farm Park, a working farm at the base of the spit that acts both as a buffer to preserve its delicate ecosystem and as an area of outstanding beauty in its own right. Only 2.5 km of the spit is accessible to the public and this loop walk follows the 'inside' beach (Golden Bay) and the 'outside' beach (Tasman Sea).

From the car park, walk north along the inside beach to the end of the row of pine trees. It is on this section of the walk that you are most likely to see wading birds. At the end of the pine trees, turn left and cut across the spit through farmland and swamp to the outside beach. In contrast to Golden Bay, the outside beach is a huge stretch of white sand pummelled by relentless surf. At the beach, turn left and walk down the shoreline until you see a red disc that marks the return to the car park via a narrow gully of nikau palms and across farmland. If you have time, continue further down the outside beach to the rocky cliffs at the end known as Fossil Point where fossils are clearly visible in the mudstone. Little blue penguins and fur seals are also a common sight.

2 Cape Farewell   Easy 🚶 15 minutes return

✳ Imposing cliffs tower above the most northerly point of the South Island.

➤ Access is signposted off the road to Wharariki Beach from Puponga.

This easy walk up a farm track leads to a coastal lookout point atop sea cliffs with a massive rock arch and giant sea caves pounded by the waves far below. At 40 degrees 30 minutes south, this is the most northerly part of the South Island and lies directly east of the Manawatu in the North Island.

Take some time to walk up the hills on either side of the lookout for even more spectacular views.

3 Pillar Point Lighthouse   Medium 🚶 1 hour return

✳ Magnificent views of Farewell Spit and as far north as Taranaki.

➤ Signposted off the road to Wharariki Beach from Puponga.

Following a 4WD track of loose stones and rock through wind-stunted manuka, this track is a steady uphill walk to a modern and rather ordinary lighthouse. The views, however, are fantastic and give the best overview of the geography of the region. To the west is Cape Farewell, directly north Farewell Spit curves far out into the sea, while to the east lie Golden and Tasman Bays. On a very clear day, Taranaki is just visible.

Some concrete foundations just below the lighthouse are all that remain of a radar station established here during the Second World War.

4 Wharariki Beach   Easy   🚶 1 hour return

❋ Wind- and sea-sculpted rock formations and seals are features of this wild West Coast beach.

➤ At Puponga, where the road turns left from the sea, proceed straight ahead (the road to the spit is to the right) and continue 5 km to the car park at the end.

The walk to Wharariki Beach is mainly through farmland with a small remnant of coastal bush near the beach. Facing the turbulent Tasman Sea, Wharariki stands in direct contrast to the sheltered Golden Bay to the east. This beautiful wide sandy beach is flanked by dramatic rock formations blasted into shape by the wave action driven by fierce and relentless westerly winds.

Keep an eye out for fur seals that like to roll in the sand and then blend right in. The beach is not safe for swimming.

Abel Tasman National Park

At just over 22,000 hectares, Abel Tasman is New Zealand's smallest national park, and in recent years has gained a reputation as being one of the most crowded during December through to February. At the same time, the combination of lush bush, spectacular coastline, crystal-clear water and breathtaking beaches makes this park hard to resist. The term 'golden' used to describe its sandy beaches does not do their colour justice, though in fact Golden Bay takes its name from early gold strikes in the district and not from the colour of the sand. An area around Tonga Island was created a marine reserve in 1993.

The Department of Conservation Great Walk is a 51-km long coastal track of mainly easy walking, linking a series of stunningly beautiful beaches with some of the best coastal scenery in the country. Unfortunately, it is also one of the most popular, and by New Zealand standards, congested in the busy summer months. However, if crowds bother you, don't be put off walking in this area – just plan a trip outside the mid-December to mid-March period (though you are unlikely to have the track entirely to yourself even then).

The two main access points are at Marahau at the southern end, and Totaranui (via Takaka) to the north, but all of the track is easily accessible by water taxi so you can create your own short walk at any point along its length. Most water taxis are based at Marahau and Kaiteriteri near Motueka, so this is a good option if you don't want to drive all the way to Totaranui, and you get to take in the magnificent coastal scenery on the way as well.

5 Abel Tasman National Park: Totaranui

✷ A beautiful beach with visitor facilities in the heart of the park.

➤ 30 km east of Takaka, road unsealed, narrow and winding beyond Wainui Inlet.

With a huge camping ground, an information centre and a boat ramp at the northern end, Totaranui offers two short walks: one heading north, the other south.

Anapai Bay   Easy   🚶 1 hour 40 minutes return

On an excellent track, the walk north to Anapai Bay begins on the flat, skirting the estuary and an open grass area with an old homestead, testament to a time when the land around Totaranui was once farmed. The track then climbs a short uphill section over a headland, beyond which it follows a gully thick with native bush including rimu, rata and beech. Anapai itself is a lovely pristine beach with dark golden sand and stunningly clear water ideal for swimming.

Goat Bay and Waiharakeke Bay   Easy

🚶 Skinners Point: 30 minutes return

Goat Bay: 40 minutes return

Waiharakeke Bay: 2 hours return

From the southern end of Totaranui, a good track follows the coast to Skinners Point where there is a fine lookout spot over the long stretch of golden sand that is Totaranui Beach to the north and Goat Bay to the south.

Goat Bay is a small sandy beach backed by native bush and perfect for swimming. Waiharakeke is a much longer beach with deep golden sand and the lush subtropical bush for which this area is justifiably famous.

6 Abel Tasman National Park: Coquille Bay *

Easy 🚶 2 hours return

---

* ✴ The most accessible attractive beach from the southern entrance to the park.

* ➤ The walk begins at the car park by the café at the northern end of Marahau township, 17 km north of Motueka.

At the southern entrance to Abel Tasman National Park, this walk is a good option for those wanting to experience the park without the long drive to Totaranui.

The track begins at the wide estuary of the Marahau River. The estuary is very tidal, as is the first beach, Tinline Bay, though this does attract a good number of wading birds. From Tinline, the track crosses a low ridge and then drops to Coquille Bay, a sheltered sandy beach backed by dense native bush and ideal for swimming.

The bay is named after the ship the *Coquille* sailed by the French navigator Dumont d'Urville, who arrived in the northern part of the South Island in early 1828.

7 Abel Tasman National Park: Wainui Falls

Easy 🚶 1 hour return

---

* ✴ A spectacular bush walk to a thundering 20-metre-high waterfall.

* ➤ From Takaka, take the road to Totaranui. At the Wainui Inlet, a clearly marked road sign to the right leads to the falls.

Beginning through farmland with a couple of shallow stream crossings that require a bit of rock hopping, the track then enters lush bush as the valley narrows, following the stream all the way to the falls. This part of the track is actually within Abel Tasman National Park, and the mature native bush is a fine mix of beech, rata and nikau. The boulder-strewn stream is impressive in its own right, with huge water-worn rocks the size of small trucks littering its length. The falls themselves thunder over a 20-metre-drop into a deep shady pool, keeping the rocks around its edge perpetually wet and consequently a bit slippery, so take care.

The track is in good condition, though the wire suspension bridge might be a bit challenging for those a little unsteady on their feet.

8 Abel Tasman Memorial   Easy   人 15 minutes

✳ A memorial to Abel Tasman with fine views over Golden Bay.

➤ On the seaward side of Abel Tasman Drive, between Pohara and Ligar Bay.

In December 1640, Dutch explorer Abel Janszoon Tasman arrived off the coast near Wainui in two ships: the *Heemskerck* and the *Zeehaen*. Unfortunately, the stay proved both short and unpleasant when a clash with local Maori resulted in the death of four of his sailors. Naming the area Moordenaars (Murderers) Bay and the country Staten Landt (later changed by a Dutch cartographer to New Zealand), Tasman never set foot on land and departed from these shores in early January.

The simple memorial to Abel Tasman and the four crewmen who died here is set on a high bluff with great views over Golden Bay. You can return to the road by the narrow concrete path to the left that leads to the further lookout with views far to the west.

9 Grove Scenic Reserve   Easy   人 30 minutes return

✳ A magical fairy-tale forest.

➤ On the road from Takaka township to Pohara Beach, the reserve is signposted from Clifton.

This tiny bush reserve is a marvellous combination of huge weathered limestone rocks, twisted old rata trees and secret pathways that feels like a forest from a children's storybook. Best of all, a narrow cleft through towering rocks leads to a lookout high above Golden Bay.

10 Te Waikoropupu (Pupu) Springs   Easy

✳ A huge natural spring with water claimed to be the clearest in the world.

➤ Take SH60, 4 km west of Takaka, and after crossing the Takaka River turn left and continue for a further 2.5 km.

人 Springs: 25 minutes return
Loop walk: 40 minutes

The springs are not actually a single outlet, but a series of eight interconnected vents in the main pool that discharge up to 14,000 litres per second at a constant temperature of 11.7 degrees Celsius. The water is a mixture of salt and fresh water as the huge underground system encompassing an area twice the size of Lake Rotorua extends out under the sea. A nifty underwater mirror system allows a peek at life below the surface.

The walk is on an excellent track through bush that includes some fine old totara and rimu trees, the remains of gold diggings from the late nineteenth century, and a surprising number of native birds. The loop walk is only a few minutes extra and you are most likely to see more native birds on this section.

11 Paynes Ford Walk   Easy   Allow 1 hour return

* Dramatic limestone cliffs tower above the Takaka River.

➤ The walk begins from the car park by the Paynes Ford Bridge, 3 km south of Takaka.

An old coach road skirts spectacular limestone bluffs along the Takaka River, creating an easy walking track, though it is a bit muddy towards the end. A maze of rough tracks created by rock climbers, with whom this area is exceptionally popular, is also worth exploring as the tracks lead to sheer cliff faces, rocky overhangs and clefts in the limestone bluffs. None are well formed though, and it can be a bit of a scramble at times. There is an erratic numbering system that must mean something to someone, but there isn't any information regarding the numbers. 'Number Four' leads up a short track to a cliff face where a rare native forget-me-not is growing.

Along the track is a swampy piece of ground that is home to the Rene Orchidston Collection of flax – so just when you thought all flax was the same, this collection will make you think again. While there is no official 'end' to this track, once you reach the bend in the river the walk becomes a lot less interesting, so it's best to return from this point.

Takaka Hill Road

This winding road between Tasman and Golden Bays has both spectacular views and fascinating geology. Famous for its distinct marble, stone was quarried from the area to build Nelson Cathedral, as well as both the old Parliament Buildings and the Beehive.

The following walks are ordered travelling from Motueka to Takaka.

12 Riwaka Resurgence Easy 人 25 minutes return

✳ Where the Riwaka Stream emerges from the base of Takaka Hill.

➤ The Resurgence is clearly marked to the left at the very base of Takaka Hill on the Motueka side. The track begins at the end of this road.

Not quite as dramatic as it sounds but a picturesque spot nonetheless, a short bush walk through mature beech leads to the base of a cliff from where the crystal-clear waters of the Riwaka Stream emerge from beneath Takaka Hill, after flowing underground for 4 km. The cave is popular with divers, who can penetrate the stream system for up to 800 metres, reaching a giant chamber with limestone formations.

There is a pleasant picnic spot by the car park.

13 Hawkes Lookout Easy 人 10 minutes return

✳ Awesome views over Tasman Bay from a marble outcrop.

➤ On the Takaka Hill road, 20 km from Motueka.

A short easy walk through a bush and rock landscape leads to a marble outcrop high above the Riwaka Valley with sweeping views over Tasman Bay towards Nelson. The Riwaka Resurgence lies in the valley directly below the lookout. As well as fine prospects east over Tasman Bay, the nearby Ngarua caves with limestone formations and a complete moa skeleton found in the system are worth a visit (there is an entrance fee).

14 Harwoods Hole/Gorge Creek Lookout

Easy   🚶   1½ hours

✹ The deepest vertical cave in New Zealand.

➤ From the Takaka Hill road, 21 km from Motueka turn right into Canaan Road and follow this unsealed, rough, narrow road for 10 km to the car park at the end.

Harwoods Hole is a colossal tomo over 170 metres deep and is the deepest vertical cave shaft in the country. The hole wasn't properly explored until December 1958, and the following month, the Starlight cave, which leads from the bottom of the hole, was also discovered.

The track is easy walking through beech forest, although the first section among moss-covered boulders is strangely devoid of ground-cover plants. Near the hole, the track is a bit of a rocky scramble, while the edge is a jumble of boulders that require a reasonable degree of fitness to negotiate. It is actually hard to see into the hole but soaring cliffs on all sides give a very good idea of its extent. There are no barriers – so if you slip, you're history! Cavers regularly use the hole, so resist the temptation to throw rocks into the shaft.

A short side track leads up to the Gorge Creek lookout located on top of a sheer escarpment with views over Gorge Creek and back towards the hole, giving a much better idea of the size of this gigantic tomo. Keep an eye out for tomtit, kakariki and robins while you're in the bush.

15 Harwoods Lookout   Easy   🚶   5 minutes return

✹ An excellent outlook and a good geology lesson as well.

➤ On the left, just below the summit on the Takaka side of the hill.

A 2-minute walk from the road, this lookout has great views over Takaka, Golden Bay as far as Farewell Spit, and west to the Lockett and Devil Ranges. Information boards detailing the geology and ecology of the region make the stop even more worthwhile.

Buller

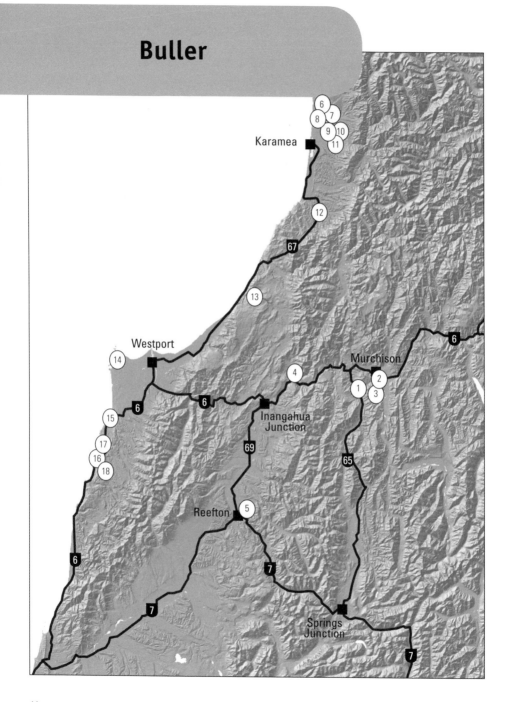

1 Maruia Falls   Easy   🚶   10 minutes

* ✳ A waterfall formed by the abrupt movement of the 1929 Murchison earthquake.

* ➤ On SH65, 11 km from the junction with SH6 west of Murchison.

The most significant remaining feature of the 1929 Murchison earthquake, the falls were created by a sharp 1-metre drop across the Maruia River. The rushing water has since eroded the riverbed further, so the falls are much higher than in 1929, and are today a popular drop for the more adventurous kayakers. There is a lookout by the car park, but you will be rewarded with a much better view by taking the short walk down to the river.

2 Skyline Walk, Murchison   Medium   🚶   1¼ hours return

* ✳ Great views over three rivers and the town of Murchison.

* ➤ Matakitaki West Bank Road, just off SH6, 1 km south of the town over the bridge.

This is a steady uphill walk on an excellent track with a moderate rather than steep grade. The lower part of the track is through beech forest and then emerges into open regenerating bush to a lookout point over the valley. If you have had enough uphill climbing, you can return from this point. From the lookout, the track continues upward to a ridge where it levels off and reaches another lookout point. The views are mainly to the north and west overlooking Murchison, the meeting of the Buller, Matiri and Matakitaki rivers, and beyond that the mountains.

3 Six Mile Power Station   Easy   🚶   1¼ hours return

* ✳ New Zealand's oldest hydro power station, set amidst beautiful beech forest.

* ➤ Turn off SH6 into Fairfax Street (where the museum is) and continue down the Matakitaki Valley for 10 km. The walk begins to the left of the tiny powerhouse.

Commissioned in 1922 and operating until 1975, Six Mile is New Zealand's oldest hydro power station. What makes this walk unique is that most of the infrastructure is still in place, including the well-preserved but tiny powerhouse. Located at the beginning of the walk, its equipment appears in such good working order that it looks as if it would start today with the mere push of a button.

From the powerhouse, the walk follows the intake pipe up a short hill to the water race. An unmarked short loop to the left through blackberry leads to the holding pond at the end of the water race. Here the walk enters beech forest thick with moss leading to the water race intake by a small weir on the Matakitaki River. The return loop track parallels the main track and continues to follow the water race high above the river back to the beginning.

4 Lyell Creek   Easy

✳ Serene forest walks through the remains of an old gold-mining settlement.

➤ In the Upper Buller Gorge, 16 km north of Inangahua on SH6.

🚶 Lyell Cemetery: 15 minutes return
     Croesus Battery and the Old Dray Road: 1½ hours

A township quickly sprang up when gold was discovered in Lyell Creek in 1862 and by 1873 included a school, post office, church and six hotels. While other gold towns have disappeared under gorse and blackberry, at Lyell the bush looks pristine and untouched and the creek runs swift and clear, and yet this valley was once home to thousands and bustling with activity. Excellent information boards in the car park feature numerous historic photographs showing the flourishing town in the late nineteenth century.

It is a short walk to the spooky Gothic cemetery where crumbling old headstones enclosed by rusting wrought-iron railings are laid out on a hillside like a quintessential horror movie graveyard. From the cemetery, the track continues through beech forest to Croesus Battery where the old stamper and other bits of machinery still remain on the bank of the creek. Returning from the battery, take the Old Dray Road track to the right, which continues down the stream and emerges just below the car park. While most of the track is in excellent condition, there are some rough patches on the Old Dray Road track due to slips in this steep and wet terrain.

A large grassed area by the car park is ideal for picnics and camping, though the usual warning about sandflies applies. Worth a look just south of Lyell is the historic Iron Bridge (built 1890), towering over 30 metres above the Buller River on massive stone pylons.

5 Golden Fleece Battery Easy k 15 minutes return

✳ Remnants of an old stamper battery beside a small gold-mining museum.

⟩ At the Murray Creek goldfields, 2 km east of Reefton.

The area around Murray Creek just east of Reefton (nicknamed 'Quartzopolis') witnessed feverish activity from 1866 until the 1920s when the supply appeared exhausted. At its peak, seven stamper batteries operated pounding ore in a bid to extract the elusive metal. Coal then replaced gold and eventually, in the 1960s, those mines also closed. Today, Reefton's fortunes are being revived with a new gold mine under way in the area.

From the Murray Creek car park, the track leads up through a mix of native and exotic trees and then down to a creek where it crosses over a footbridge built on the foundations of the original Golden Fleece battery. The track then follows the old water pipe to the battery. Although the original battery no longer exists, the old Morning Star battery has been reconstructed on the site and is one of only a few stamper batteries still in operation. Right next to it is the small Blacks Point Museum, dedicated to gold mining in the area and surrounded by a fascinating collection of old machinery.

Buller

Kahurangi National Park

At over 450,000 hectares, Kahurangi is a huge park, and mostly only accessible by tracks that require both stamina and time. Traversing the heart of the park, the 82-km Heaphy Track offers a great range of landscapes from the tussock-clad Gouland Downs crossing through to lush subtropical forest complete with nikau palms at the Karamea end of the walk. The following three short walks along the coast just north of Karamea are a small taste of both the Heaphy Track and Kahurangi National Park.

6 Kahurangi National Park: Scotts Beach
Easy k 2 hours return

✳ Undemanding trek to spectacular white-sand surf beach with camping facilities.

⟩ From Karamea township, head north along the coast for 15 km to the southern end of the Heaphy Track at the Kohaihai River.

This well-maintained section of the Heaphy Track to Scotts Beach is so beautifully graded that you will hardly raise a sweat on the initial uphill section to Scotts Lookout. But think twice before making the lookout your sole destination, as the views are at best very modest. On the downhill stretch from the lookout, Scotts Beach comes into view quickly, though it is still quite a way to reach it. The beach itself is a stunning stretch of white sand backed by luxuriant bush, but the thundering surf makes it too dangerous for swimming. However, there is a sheltered grassy picnic area with toilets and fireplaces just back from the beach, and you can also camp here.

7 Kahurangi National Park: Nikau Walk

Easy 𝄇 40 minutes return

* A touch of the tropics in the South Island, with black fantails flitting among luxuriant nikau groves.

➤ This walk branches off the beginning of the Heaphy Track to the right, after crossing the swing bridge over the Kohaihai River, not far from the car park.

As the name suggests, this walk loops through swathes of nikau palm, but the massive southern rata along the track are also spectacular. Ngaio and karaka, at their southern growing limit, are also present, and jet-black fantails are common too. There is a shorter 10-minute loop that can easily be tacked on to the walk to Scotts Beach.

8 Kahurangi National Park: Zigzag Track

Hard 𝄇 25 minutes return

* Non-stop views right the way up to a superb panorama of river and coastline.

➤ This track also branches off to the right at the beginning of the Heaphy Track, but before the Kohaihai River crossing.

Zigzag it says, and zigzag it is! A short but relentless uphill grind to a lookout point high above the coast through open vegetation reveals continuous views all the way, and from the top are excellent perspectives of the Kohaihai River and beach.

Top Isolated sandy beaches fringed by luxuriant bush are the high point of several short walks in Abel Tasman National Park.

Above Farewell Spit, the largest recurved sand spit in the world, is home to a vast number of seabirds including Australasian gannets.

Left above Rugged cliffs and a giant rock arch distinguish Cape Farewell, the most northerly point of the South Island.

Left below Rarangi Beach stretches along the shores of Cloudy Bay from the short walk to Monkey Bay.

Below The Oparara River flows gently through the low arch of Moria Gate north of Karamea.

Opposite A swing bridge over the Kohaihai River (above) marks the beginning of the walk to Scotts Beach (below) on the Heaphy Track.

Above Perched high above Cape Foulwind, this lookout provides an up-close view of the fur seal colony.

Left Remains of a stamper battery lie deep in the beech forest at Lyell.

Opposite At Ross, check out the inmate in the jail (above) at the beginning of the Ross Water Race walkway. The views from the historic cemetery (below) are over Ross town and the opencast gold mine, which has only recently closed down.

Above The Rangitane Walk along the Arnold River, the outlet of Lake Brunner, has spectacular views over the lake and profuse native bush.

Left At Nelson Creek, access to the old goldfields, with their deep water races, is through a handmade tunnel and then over a suspension bridge.

Opposite top The Christchurch Botanic Gardens are nestled within a loop of the Avon River in Hagley Park.

Opposite bottom Like Lyttelton Harbour, Akaroa on the Banks Peninsula is the crater of an old volcano, and the rugged hills and secluded bays make for great walks.

Top From the Haast Pass Lookout, mountain views unfold both east and west along the pass.
Above A swing bridge over the clear rushing waters of the Makarora River is all part of the
fun on the walk to the Blue Pools in the Haast Pass.

Oparara Basin

The bird life amongst the magnificent virgin bush and fascinating limestone landscapes of the Oparara River valley is prolific, and there is a good chance of spotting the rare blue duck, the whio, which makes its home on swift-flowing river systems. The road into the basin, however, is a challenge: narrow, winding, unsealed and with stretches where it is difficult to pass. A Department of Conservation sign at the beginning advises that the road is unsuitable for caravans and campervans, though short-wheel-based campervans will manage the route.

Car parks are the starting points for the three shorter walks that follow. Weka are common in the vicinity so keep a close eye on your belongings as they are cheeky enough to jump on in if you leave a door open.

9 Oparara Arch   Easy   🚶 40 minutes return

* Colossal natural arches over the Oparara River.

➤ From Karamea, drive north for 10 km, then turn right into McCallums Mill Road and follow the narrow, unsealed road for a further 15 km to the car park.

Reputed to be the largest natural arch in New Zealand, there are in fact two arches over the Oparara River and huge limestone cliffs enclose both. The main arch is over 200 metres long and the river flows through it. Although you are unable to walk through, a viewpoint allows a peek to the other side. The second arch is gigantic and towers far above the river. It is so massive and yet appears so fragile that it feels uncomfortable to stand beneath. An added attraction is that the walk to the arches is along a beautiful stony river and through virgin beech forest.

10 Moria Gate   Easy   🚶 1 hour return

* A more up-close and personal encounter with a natural rock arch.

➤ This walk also begins from the McCallums Mill Road car park.

In direct comparison to the grandiose Oparara Arch, Moria Gate is lower and far more delicate. The walk proceeds through mature beech forest dripping with moss, and the actual access to the arch is through a small side cave which is a bit of a scramble, but chain ropes help. From the cave, you emerge onto a sandy ledge right inside the arch itself with both ends visible. The rocks within the cave have a dimpled pattern from the action of water over the years, and if the level is low you can wade upstream for a view of the arch from outside.

If you're in the mood for a longer walk, the track continues on to Mirror Tarn and then joins the road for a short stretch back to the car park.

11 Crazy Paving and Box Canyon Caves
Easy 人 20 minutes return

✳ Unique cave experiences featuring our only indigenous cave spider.

➤ The car park for these caves is 2 km beyond the Oparara Arches car park.

The name of the first cave comes from the patterns on its floor, formed by mud that has over time dried and shrunk, cracking into these patterns. This cave is also home to New Zealand's only cave spider, and while the elusive arachnid is not visible, the delicate egg sacs hanging from the roof are clear to see. Just a little further along, and accessed by steps, is Box Canyon Cave, a large roomy cave deep in the limestone hill.

The short walk to the caves is through beautiful beech forest and a torch is necessary for both. Information boards with separate text for both adults and children are very much appreciated.

12 Lake Hanlon   Easy 人 30 minutes return

✳ A quick walk to a small bush-fringed lake.

➤ 20 km south of Karamea, on SH67.

Formed by the 1929 Murchison earthquake, this picturesque little lake lies below the Karamea Bluffs. There is a good chance of seeing curious weka scuttling in the undergrowth alongside the excellent beech-forest track.

13 Charming Creek Easy

✳ A fascinating combination of human and natural history, following an old railway line to the Mangatini Falls.

➤ At Ngakawau, on SH67, turn into Tylers Road just before the bridge over the Ngakawau River.

🚶 Mangatini Falls: 1¾ hours return

Watson Mill: 2 hours return

One of the best short walks in the country, this walk mingles superb natural scenery such as the Mangatini Falls and the Ngakawau Gorge, with the more appealing man-made features such as old railway tunnels and a swing bridge.

This private railway was opened in 1914 to bring coal down from the Charming Creek Mine, but was also used to extract timber. Finally closed in 1958, most of the line is still intact, as are the three tunnels. The old bridge foundations still remain too, as well as the foundations of the 'bins' (an area used for sorting coal). More recent slips and rock falls illustrate what a daunting task it must have been to both build and maintain this track. The bush along the way is luxurious, and glow-worms are a feature of the tunnels and some of the railway cuttings.

The Mangatini Falls tumble down a side stream into the Ngakawau River, and the rare daisy *Celmisia morganii* at their base is found only in the Ngakawau Gorge (most *Celmisia* are alpine plants).

Beyond the falls, the track goes through a tunnel to Watson Mill, a pleasant picnic spot at the confluence of the Ngakawau River and Charming Creek, and the old site of a timber mill.

As the walkway follows the railway line, it is for the most part flat; and if you intend to do the whole walk it will take about 3 hours one-way.

14 Cape Foulwind

✳ A lighthouse and seal colony, at either end of the Cape Foulwind walkway.

➤ From Westport head south, and just over the Buller River turn right into Cape Foulwind Road. It is 12 km to the lighthouse and a further 5 km to the seal colony at Tauranga Bay. If you are heading south from the seal colony, you can take Watsons Lead Road, which joins SH6, 16 km north of Charleston.

Cape Foulwind Lighthouse   Easy   🚶   20 minutes return

The walkway around Cape Foulwind takes around 1½ hours one-way, though the short walks from either end access the more interesting sections. A rather ordinary-looking structure has replaced the older wooden lighthouse built in 1876 on the high cliffs of the cape. The best coastal views are from the base of the lighthouse and look far to the north over Westport and beyond to the Karamea Bluffs. The mischievous weka is common around the car park.

Seal Colony and Tauranga Bay   Easy   🚶   20 minutes return

Tauranga Bay is a broad surf beach sheltered by headlands at either end. The seal colony is on the northern headland together with a small offshore island and is just a short walk up from the car park. This is a great spot to watch fur seals as the lookout point is directly above the colony with its numerous rock pools, which make an ideal seal playground. The number of seals varies with the season, though the best time to see pups is between December and March. However, keep a sharp eye out, as seals can be hard to spot and are not confined to the colony: there may be more of them here than you at first think. A heavy swell makes this walk even more dramatic.

15 Constant and Joyce Bays Lookout and Loop Walk
Easy   🚶   30 minutes return

* ✳ Excellent coastal views from a rocky headland.

* ➤ Turn off SH6 down Princes Street, Charleston (almost opposite the Charleston pub).

The goldfields and most of the town of Charleston have long disappeared under regrowth masking the frenetic activity that made the settlement a boom town after gold was discovered here in August 1866. By October of that year the population had risen to 1200, and by 1869 to almost 20,000. In its heyday, the town supported 80 hotels, three breweries and even a casino: 'Casino De Venice'. Robert Hannah opened his first shoe shop in Charleston (now the Hannahs footwear chain), and when the postmaster was moved from Wellington to Charleston it was considered a promotion! Today, only one pub and a handful of houses remain.

Joyce and Constant Bays are two small coves below the town. The track starts from the car park by the toilets and winds through gorse and flax to a headland with views to the north as far as Cape Foulwind. If you're very lucky you might spot a pod of the rare Hector's dolphin offshore, and the bays are also the breeding grounds of blue penguins.

Punakaiki Coast

A stunning combination of sea, beautiful bush and fabulous rock formations, Punakaiki is more than just the Pancake Rocks and Blowhole. There are a number of excellent short walks, good accommodation and cafés, and the road along the coast is spectacular in its own right.

16 Truman Track   Easy   🚶   30 minutes return

* ✳ From forest to a dramatic rocky coast, this short track has it all.

* ➤ On SH6, 2 km north of Pancake Rocks.

The Truman Track is a flat, well-formed path that winds through a mature forest of matai, rimu and rata to a short coastal strip of flax, and finally down to a small sandy cove (not safe for swimming). There are impressive views along this rugged mountainous coastline and at low tide it is possible to explore the sea caves and the rocky shore. Blue penguins nest here from August to February and the best viewing times are around dawn and dusk.

17 Pororari Gorge Lookout   Easy   🚶   40 minutes return

* ✳ Dense rainforest lines the river along this deep limestone gorge.

* ➤ 1.5 km north of Punakaiki on SH6.

Limestone cliffs rise high above the Pororari River as it twists its way through a deep gorge to the sea. Lush bush thick with ferns, kiekie and nikau palms overhang the track, giving it a distinctive tropical feel. The track begins under the Pororari River Bridge and is flat all the way to the lookout, which has views deep into the limestone hills. The track continues further upstream, so if you feel like walking more then keep on going until you've had enough.

18 Pancake Rocks and Blowhole Easy 30 minutes return

✳ Unusual rock formations eroded over the years to form spectacular blowholes, sea caves and arches.

➤ On SH6 at Punakaiki.

Yes, you've seen it on a hundred calendars, and sure it does get crowded in summer, but when a heavy swell is running this place is spectacular. The unusual layered limestone rock formations have been formed over millions of years, and in more recent times shaped into the pancake rocks seen today. The short well-formed path wends its way above bluffs, sea caves, arches and narrow fissures in the rock that act as blowholes, and are at their most impressive at high tide or in rough weather.

Buller

Westland

Greymouth

Hokitika

Ross

Harihari

Fox Glacier

Haast

1 Nelson Creek

✳ A latticework of tunnels and deep water races in historic gold-mining territory.

➤ From SH7 north of Greymouth, turn off at Ngahere, and Nelson Creek is 7 km from the turn-off.

Gold was discovered here in 1865 but the boom was short-lived and today Nelson Creek is noted for its tunnels and deep water races. Both walks begin over the river, which is accessed first through a handmade miner's tunnel topped by an old beech tree and then over a suspension bridge to the far side of the stream.

Colls Dam   Easy   𝄃   30 minutes return

The Colls Dam loop walk through mature beech forest crosses a number of narrow, but very deep, water races and tunnels. These races took the water from Colls Dam to the river, scouring out the soft alluvial gold-bearing soils, which were then sifted in search of a fortune. While the walk includes Colls Dam itself, what appears to be a track around the dam is actually just a dead end.

Tailrace Walk   Easy   𝄃   20 minutes return

Over the suspension bridge, turn left and follow the track up a wide gully formed by sluicing and then through forest, predominantly red and silver beech. The loop walk leads back to the river, passing deep water races and an old tunnel, which can be explored. This track is rough in places.

Back at the river, there is a small side creek where you can legally fossick for gold and keep what you find. There is a large pleasant picnic area by the car park, good camping facilities, and a swimming hole in the river.

2 Rangitane Walk, Lake Brunner   Easy   𝄃   30 minutes return

✳ A combination river and lakeside walk through mature native forest.

➤ At Moana, turn right into Ahau Street and follow the road to the car park at the end by the lake edge.

Inland from Greymouth, this large tree-fringed lake is popular for boating, fishing (brown trout) and swimming. The TranzAlpine stops at Moana (which is also the Maori name for the lake), and a few hours at Lake Brunner on a good day might have more appeal than Greymouth, the train's terminus.

The walk begins across an attractive suspension bridge over the dark waters of the Arnold River, the outlet for Lake Brunner. Turning right over the bridge, the track leads through a grove of kamahi, a small tree with beautiful mottled white, grey and brown bark, the colours mixing tastefully with green mosses. The mixed podocarp forest also has large kahikatea, rimu and beech, with a ground cover of Prince of Wales fern, easily recognised by its dark and delicate feathery fronds. Kereru are common in this reserve, noisily flopping about the treetops.

The walk forms a loop with views over the river, and back at the bridge a short side track continues to the lake's western shores with views across the water to the mountains.

Greymouth

3 Brunner Mine Industrial Site Easy 人 Allow 45 minutes

* One of the country's earliest industrial sites and scene of its worst mining disaster.

➤ 12 km north of Greymouth on SH7, towards Reefton.

Thomas Brunner first discovered coal in the area in the 1840s, but it wasn't until 1864 that the first mining began, eventually leading to eight mines working in the immediate vicinity of the Grey River. A suspension bridge across the river was built in 1876, linking the mines on the north bank with transport on the south bank. In 1896 an explosion deep underground in the Brunner Mine killed 65 miners; a memorial with the names of the dead stands on the north side of the river. The mines eventually closed in 1942.

The remains of the mining activity are extensive on both sides of the river, including the impressive Tyneside chimney and beehive coke ovens. Good information boards with historical photographs make for an even more worthwhile stop.

4 Point Elizabeth Lookout   Easy 🚶 1¼ hours return

❋ Beautiful bush walk lush with nikau palms and a great coastal lookout point.

➤ From Greymouth, take the road north to Westport over the Grey River Bridge. Immediately over the bridge, turn left and follow the road along the coast 6 km to the very end.

Originally, gold miners used the beach as a highway to travel north and south, but the high cliffs of Point Elizabeth were a difficult section to cross and in 1865 this track was constructed to make access much easier.

From the road, the track climbs a short distance and then levels off and from this point on is mostly flat all the way to the lookout, with the boom of the sea almost constant along its entire length. Passing through dense groves of kiekie and nikau palm, the track traverses an area of pure flax just before the lookout. Nikau at Point Elizabeth is at its southernmost growing limit on the west coast of New Zealand, making these trees some of the most southerly naturally growing palm trees in the world.

The views from the lookout extend far to the north along this wild stretch of coast, while to the south the breakwater at Greymouth is just visible, and offshore two small rocky islands are home to numerous seabirds.

5 Coal River Heritage Park   Easy 🚶 20 minutes return

❋ A stroll along the Grey River lined with historic reminders of the gold and coal years.

➤ Start from the east end of Mawhera Quay, Greymouth.

Greymouth has long been a busy port, from the early days of gold in the 1860s, through coal, timber, fishing and now back again to coal. The Heritage Park runs along the stopbank of the Grey River from the railway station (built 1897) to the port loading area, and includes the restored Harbour Board building (1884), signal station (one of only two left in New Zealand), the dredge buckets from the *Mawhera* (built in Scotland in 1908), and old railway carriages and stock. Interpretive panels with historical photos make for an interesting short walk.

6 Londonderry Rock, Kumara   Easy   🏃 15 minutes return

✹ A massive glacial boulder sitting among historic gold tailings.

➤ 2 km west of Kumara on SH73.

This short walk through old gold diggings leads to a massive boulder left over from the glacial age. These tailings have been exposed by miners sluicing away the soil, leaving only stones and large rocks too heavy to move, and in this case one enormous boulder the size of a small truck. The area around Kumara was the site of New Zealand's last gold rush in 1876.

7 Roadside Tunnel Loop, Hokitika   Easy   🏃 20 minutes return

✹ A short access tunnel leads to a loop walk through old gold workings.

➤ From Hokitika, head north for 10 km on SH6 and turn right into the Stafford–Dillmanstown Road. The car park is on the left, 6 km down this road, and the walk starts on the opposite side of the road.

The beginning of this walk is through a short tunnel in a fern-lined bank opposite the car park and emerges under a boulder cliff into regenerating rimu and kamahi bush. The track then drops down to a creek, which disappears into another dark tunnel. Everywhere are piles of rocks left over from mining activities, and the track is lined with, and in some places constructed from, these boulders. Eventually the track loops back through another tunnel to emerge on the road a short distance from the car park. The tunnels were originally constructed to carry water to the gold diggings.

Lake Kaniere

Late autumn/early winter can be a good time to visit Westland; most of the tourists have gone, the weather is often settled with calm clear skies, and the early snow on the Southern Alps makes the views even more dramatic. Set in mature forest, 194-metre-deep Lake Kaniere is overlooked by two smaller mountains, Mt Graham (828 m), and Tuhua (1124 m) and has a number of short tracks along its shores including the following three easy walks.

8 Kahikatea Forest Walk, Lake Kaniere

Easy 🚶 10 minutes return

✳ Towering kahikatea dominate this lakeside bush walk.

➤ From Hokitika, turn off SH6 into Stafford Street and then into Lake Kaniere Road and continue on this road for 18 km. When you reach the lake turn right into Sunny Bright Road and drive the short distance to the picnic area.

This short walk begins over a boardwalk through flax, then heads into dense native bush thick with mosses and ferns and dominated by spectacularly tall kahikatea before following a pretty bush stream back to the car park.

Although the sandflies can be fierce, the picnic area is very attractive in its own right, fringed by flax and large trees and with views right down the lake to the mountains.

9 Canoe Cove, Lake Kaniere Easy 🚶 20 minutes return

✳ An airy rimu colonnade leads to a serene lakeshore prospect.

➤ The track begins 1 km north of the Sunny Bright Road turn-off, and to the left opposite Milltown Road.

In contrast to the previous walk, here rimu dominates the forest which is also much more open and light in character. The track leads down to a small beach and a quiet tree-lined backwater with peaceful views across the lake.

10 Dorothy Falls, Lake Kaniere Easy 🚶 5 minutes return

✳ A small picturesque waterfall tumbles in several drops into a bush-lined pool.

➤ 2 km past Milltown Road the seal ends and the road narrows. The Dorothy Falls are 6 km on the left past the point where the seal ends.

Set just a few minutes off the road, the elegant Dorothy Falls is a series of small drops into a bush-fringed pool, ideal for a dip on a hot day.

11 Hokitika Gorge   Easy   🚶 20 minutes return

* ✴ The turquoise waters of the Hokitika River swirl through a narrow limestone gorge 25 km east of the town.

* ➤ From SH6, take the road out towards Kokatahi, and then follow the signs to the gorge via Kowhitirangi and Whitcombe Roads.

This short 20-minute walk leads down to the stunning limestone gorge with views along the Hokitika from a swing bridge over the river. The clear rushing waters are a vivid turquoise colour and are flanked by white water-worn limestone rock, overhung by mature native trees.

12 Bellbird Walk, Lake Mahinapua   Easy   🚶 15 minutes return

* ✴ Melodious bush beside the shores of tranquil Lake Mahinapua.

* ➤ On SH6, 10 km south of Hokitika.

This small lake just south of Hokitika has a number of short walks and is also very popular with those wanting a gentle kayaking experience on a pretty, bush-enclosed waterway. There is a large picnic and camping area, and preserved by the lake edge are the remains of the Lake Mahinapua paddle steamer, built in Hokitika in 1883 to provide transport for those travelling between Hokitika and Ross.

The Bellbird Walk begins from the southern end of the camping area and is a flat loop walk through attractive bush around an old gold dredge pond. As the name suggests, bellbirds are common in the vicinity. The famous Mahinapua pub is on SH6 just north of the picnic area.

13 Ross Water Race   Easy   🚶 1 hour

* ✴ Gold workings and historic buildings in this old gold-mining town.

* ➤ The walk begins from the Ross visitors' centre. Note that while you can drive past the centre, the road is very narrow, parking is limited and it is rather difficult to turn around.

Gold was discovered at Ross in 1864, and within a year the population had burgeoned to 3000. Weighing 3 kg, the largest gold nugget ever found in New

Westland

Zealand was discovered in Jones Creek in 1909, and named 'the Honourable Roddy' after the then Minister of Mines the Honourable Roderick McKenzie. Gold continues to be extracted at Ross, the opencast mine behind the visitors' centre only closed in 2004 and new mining operations are opening up closer to the sea.

From the car park, follow the roadway up Mt Greenland Road (not steep despite the name), and follow the Jones Creek to the end of the road. It was in this very stream that the Honourable Roddy was found and you can try your hand at gold panning here too. Pans are available for hire from the friendly visitors' centre and panning is best just after heavy rain. At the end of the road, the track then leads to the right up through regenerating bush via old tunnels, a miner's cottage and the historic Ross cemetery, which has views over Ross and to the north.

Back at the visitors' centre, take time to view the old cottage, the Ross jail, a reconstructed water wheel and an old sluicing gun. You might even like to finish off with a visit to the 140-year-old Empire Hotel just down the road.

Okarito Lagoon

Okarito has outstanding views of the pristine vistas that stretch from the Tasman Sea across coastal lowland forest to the towering Southern Alps. Okarito is also the home of two rare birds, the Okarito brown kiwi and the only New Zealand breeding colony of the kotuku, or white heron. The elegant kotuku, *Egretta alba modesta*, is found throughout the South Pacific, Australia and Asia, but is rare in New Zealand, giving rise to a traditional Maori proverb, 'He kotuku rerenga tahi' – 'A kotuku of a single flight' – referring to a once-in-a-lifetime event. The kotuku is the bird featured on the two-dollar coin. The Okarito brown kiwi, now identified as a separate species, is often heard and occasionally seen on the road at night.

14 Pakihi Walk, Okarito Lagoon   Easy   𐀀   25 minutes return

✳ A commanding lookout over Okarito Lagoon, the mountains and the forests of Westland.

➤ Turn off SH6 and drive towards Okarito, and the walk begins 5 km on the right.

The track initially skirts a pakihi swamp, and then climbs gently uphill to a lookout. Snow-tipped mountains loom directly to the east, while to the west Okarito Lagoon spreads to the sea. The lookout is on top of an old glacial moraine, a hillock of debris left behind as the glaciers retreated thousands of years ago. Pakihi swamp is peculiar to the high-rainfall areas typical of the West Coast. These wetlands are almost permanently wet and are characterised by low stunted vegetation that is the result of nutrients being rapidly leached off the waterlogged soils.

15 Okarito Trig   Medium   ⋏   1¼ hours return

✳ Superb views from the sea to the mountains across untouched wilderness.

➤ From SH6, turn off to Okarito and drive 13 km to the coast. At Okarito, turn left (there is only one road) and the walk begins at the end of this road.

The views from the Okarito trig sum up everything that you have come to the West Coast to see. Initially the walk begins through bush, with the nearby surf resounding like the continuous roar of a jet engine. The uphill stretch is a solid climb but not too steep, and the reward at the top is worth the effort. Pristine forest stretches endlessly both north and south. To the south-east is Mt Elie De Beaumont and further south is Aoraki/Mt Cook and Mt Tasman with the Franz Josef Glacier tucked in below. Immediately to the north are the myriad arms of the Okarito Lagoon sliding gently into dark forest, while just to the south Three Mile Lagoon is visible, with the coastline disappearing far into the horizon.

If the weather is clear and fine, don't drive past this walk.

Fox and Franz Josef Glaciers

New Zealand is the only place in the world where glaciers reach such low levels, coming within 20 km of the sea. Both these glaciers have their own unique characteristics: Fox is set in a dramatic steep-sided glacial valley, while Franz Josef lies in a bush-clad valley and is more easily viewed from a distance. Once the glaciers stretched to the sea, but after thousands of years of warming weather are now confined to the mountains (although both are currently advancing again). From a distance, the glaciers can appear a little grubby and disappointing, but once at their face the creaking and groaning of the slowly grinding blue-green ice is awe-inspiring.

The Maori name for Franz Josef is Ka Roimata o Hinehukatere – the Tears of Hinehukatere. According to legend, Hinehukatere and her lover, Tuawe, were exploring the area when Tuawe was swept away by an avalanche and killed. The copious tears shed by Hinehukatere froze and formed the glacier. Fox Glacier is known as Te Moeka o Tuawe and is the final resting place (moeka) of Tuawe.

Short walks lead to the terminals of both glaciers and guided walks are available on the glaciers themselves. There is plenty of accommodation and cafés at both Fox and Franz Josef (the latter is the larger township), though accommodation is at a premium in the busy summer months.

16 Franz Josef Glacier   Easy

✴ Less than 10 km from the sea, Franz Josef Glacier glides down the mountain into lush bush.

➤ The glacier is signposted off SH6 just south of Franz Josef township. The walks begin at the terminal car park.

🚶 Franz Josef Terminal View: 30 minutes return

Sentinel Rock: 20 minutes return

Named by the explorer Julius von Haast in 1865 after Franz Josef, Emperor of Austria, this glacier, the more northerly of the two, is steeper and faster-moving than Fox and is more easily photographed.

The walk starts through forest and then follows the riverbed to a lookout near the terminal of the glacier. The erratic nature of the riverbed means that this track varies from season to season.

Sentinel Rock is a short uphill climb to a lookout point with great views over the glacier and valley and is a particularly good spot for taking photographs. Late afternoon with the sun setting in the west has the best light.

17 Fox Glacier   Easy   🚶 1 hour return

✴ Fox Glacier lies at the head of a rock-strewn valley ripped apart by the power of moving ice.

➤ Turn off SH6 just south of Fox Glacier village.

In contrast to Franz Josef, Fox lies in a shattered valley torn apart by ice, with cliffs shorn clean by its relentless movement. The walk to the terminal is worthwhile just to appreciate the sheer power and force of this glacier, but it is dangerous to walk on the ice or directly up to the terminal without a guide. The ice is extremely unstable and constantly melting and moving, and several recent accidents have occurred when people have ventured beyond the barriers.

18 Lake Matheson   Easy   ⅄   1½ hours

✳ A small lake perfectly reflects the nearby mountains in its tranquil waters.

➤ 5 km west of Fox Glacier township.

Known as a 'kettle lake', Lake Matheson was formed by a large section of ice left behind when Fox Glacier retreated from its last advance, around 14,000 years ago, and the depression created by the melting ice filled with water. Possibly the most photographed lake in New Zealand, Lake Matheson is famous for the mirror image of Cook, Tasman and La Perouse mountains reflected in its still waters. The best time for photographing the reflection is early morning before the wind gets up and ruffles the surface.

Even if you aren't a morning person, the loop walk is still an attractive stroll around the kahikatea- and rimu-fringed lake with the snow-topped mountains in the distance.

19 Munro Beach   Easy   ⅄   1½ hours return

✳ A small wild beach that is home to the rare Fiordland crested penguin.

➤ Off SH6, 30 km north of Haast at the southern end of Lake Moeraki.

Munro Beach is a small sandy cove flanked by rocky headlands and pounded by the wild weather straight off the Tasman Sea. This beach is home to fur seals and the very rare Fiordland crested penguin. Only 1500 pairs remain, and like most penguins they are somewhat timid. The best time to see them is early morning or late afternoon, and it is best to sit still rather than wander all over the beach.

From the car park, you have two choices to access the track. The 4WD track that leads straight ahead is shorter but you have to wade across the stream and you'll get your feet wet. The longer – and dryer – way via a bridge leads from the northern side of the car park and both tracks meet up just a short distance from the beginning. In addition to the beautiful beach, the walk down to the sea goes through attractive mature bush with towering rimu overhead.

20 Ship Creek

✳ Swamp and dune contrast on two unmissable short coastal walks.

➤ On SH6, 15 km north of Haast.

Kahikatea Swamp Walk   Easy   ⅄   20 minutes

From the car park, this walk crosses back under the highway and follows Ship Creek through thick forest to a small loop through a kahikatea swamp. Mainly on raised boardwalks, this section of the walk has a 'Southern Gothic' feel with massive ancient trees, heavy with mosses, creepers and lichens, rising straight out of the dark murky waters, heavily stained with plant tannin. These are kahikatea at their most impressive.

Dune Lake Walk   Easy   ⅄   30 minutes

This walk is much more open in character than its companion walk and starts out along the beach, leading to a lookout tower atop a dune. The view south along the beach stretches all the way to Jackson Head, 50 km down the coast, while inland it extends over dune country backed by the splendid mountains of the Southern Alps.

From the lookout, the track then skirts a small lake fringed by reeds before finally looping back through rimu forest to the starting point. Considering its proximity to the sea, the bush is amazingly lush. It is also worth spending some time down on the beach here, with water-worn driftwood lining the sand and the air heavy with salt spray from the wild surf.

21 Hapuka Estuary   Easy   🚶 20 minutes return

* Three distinct ecosystems in just one short loop walk.

➤ From Haast, head south along the coast towards Jackson Bay for 15 km. The walk begins on the left, 2 km after crossing the bridge over the Okuru River.

This short flat walk encompasses three interlinked ecosystems of forest, wetlands and estuary. Starting through bush dominated by rimu and kahikatea, the first section of the walk is dense with the semi-climbing plant kiekie that gives the bushscape a distinctive subtropical feel. Some of the rimu here are estimated to be between 500 and 800 years old. Emerging from the shade, a raised boardwalk traverses a wetland thick with flax and manuka, and then finally the track follows the river bank of the estuary back to the car park. The dark tea-coloured water is overhung with old kowhai trees, and whitebait are prolific in these tidal waters during the season.

Westland

Haast Pass Road

The road through the Haast Pass follows an ancient Maori trail called Tiora Patea ('the way is clear'), used to access pounamu on the West Coast, and at 563 metres it is the lowest pass through the Southern Alps. Gold prospector Charles Cameron was the first European to use the pass in 1863, followed a few weeks later by the explorer Julius von Haast, after whom it was named.

Although used extensively as the most direct route from Dunedin to the West Coast goldfields and later as a cattle trail, serious work on improving the road did not begin until 1929. The road (145 km from Haast to Wanaka; 80 km from Haast to Makarora) is now sealed and only rarely blocked by snow, and goes through the heart of Mt Aspiring National Park. Haast township, originally a workers' camp for the Ministry of Works, has very limited accommodation and facilities.

22 Roaring Billy   Easy   🚶 25 minutes return

* This stream rushes down a series of cascades into the Haast River.

➤ On SH6, 27 km from Haast.

A level walk through beautiful beech forest dense with mosses and ferns takes you to the edge of the Haast River, at this point a wide gravel riverbed. This is the wettest part of the road, with rain falling on average 180 days a year and with an annual fall of over 5500 mm. The Roaring Billy is a tributary of the Haast and at this juncture crashes down a series of boulder-strewn cascades into the river. Walk across the riverbed for a better view of the stream that is particularly spectacular after heavy rain.

23 Thunder Creek Falls Easy 🚶 5 minutes return

✳ A 28-metre waterfall dropping into the Haast River.

➤ On SH6, 51 km from Haast.

A short walk through beech forest to the Thunder Creek Falls, which plunges in a single drop of nearly 30 metres from a glacial hanging valley into the Haast River.

24 Fantail Creek Falls Easy 🚶 5 minutes return

✳ A picturesque waterfall across the Haast River.

➤ On SH6, 57 km from Haast.

Although the waterfall is easily seen from the road, it is worth the short 5-minute walk to the edge of the fast-flowing Haast River for a closer view of this pretty fan-shaped waterfall on the other side.

25 Haast Pass Lookout Hard 🚶 40 minutes return

✳ A prime lookout down the pass in both directions.

➤ On SH6, 61 km from Haast.

This new track zigzags up through beech forest that gradually thins as you climb and finally reaches a lookout over the pass. The view down the bush-lined pass extends both east and west and snowcapped mountains soar in every direction. It is a bit of slog but the track is well formed, so take your time as the views are well worth the effort.

26 Camerons Creek Easy 🚶 20 minutes return

✳ A lofty lookout over the Makarora River valley.

➤ On SH6, 68 km from Haast.

This short walk leads through beech forest to a wooden platform high over the Makarora River with views along the mountains and valley to the west. The creek is named after the first European to traverse the pass in 1863, Charles Cameron.

27 Blue Pools Easy 🚶 30 minutes return

✳ Trout swim lazily in these deep clear pools alongside the Makarora River.

➤ On SH6, 72 km from Haast.

At the confluence of the Blue and Makarora rivers a series of pools of deep clear water, overhung by beech forest, vary in colour between blue and green (either colour water is very cold at any time of the year). Keep an eye out for enormous brown and rainbow trout both at the pools and in the river by the swing bridge. The trout are more common in winter when they come upstream to spawn. The easy walk on a good track is through handsome virgin beech forest.

28 Makarora Easy 🚶 15 minutes return

✳ A primeval forest of mature native trees and home to native birds.

➤ 80 km east of Haast and 65 km west of Wanaka on SH6.

The dense primeval forest around Makarora contrasts dramatically with the dry landscape only a few kilometres to the east. These flats were once forested in beech, matai, kahikatea and miro, and the township of Makarora grew as a milling centre supplying the Otago goldfields with much-needed timber.

A hundred metres west of the Makarora visitors' centre, the short flat walk passes through a small remnant of this great forest and includes an old pit for hand-sawing logs still complete with the saw. Despite its small size the forest supports a good number of native birds including the elusive kaka.

North Canterbury, Kaikoura, including Lewis Pass

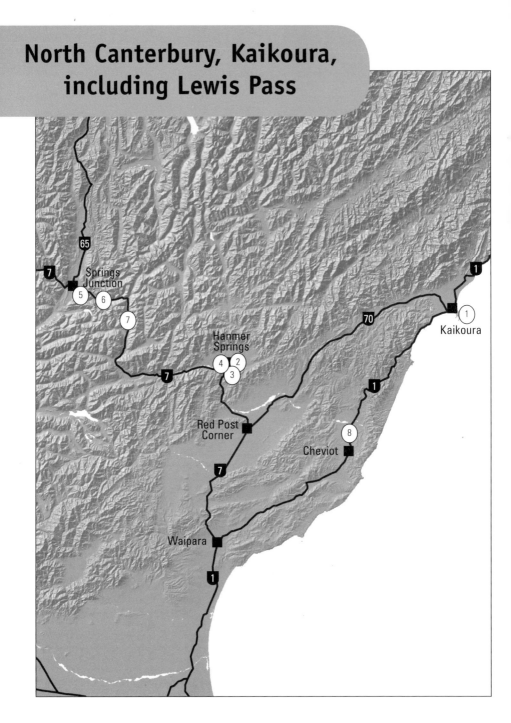

Kaikoura

The physical location of Kaikoura is nothing short of spectacular. Within a short distance of the coast the rugged Kaikoura mountains rise to nearly 3000 metres, and offshore the seabed drops steeply into the Hikurangi Trench, also known as the Kaikoura Canyon. The mountains are some of the most recent in New Zealand, formed less than 200,000 years ago during a period of rapid uplift. In recent years the town has flourished with the advent of whale watching, outgrowing the small town centre sheltered beneath the peninsula and spreading northwards.

1 Kaikoura Walkway and Seal Colony   Easy

* ✷ Coastal and mountain views from a peninsula steeped in Maori and European history.

* ➤ All four walks begin at Point Kean at the eastern end of the peninsula.

* ⚐ Lookout Point: 10 minutes return

  Whalers Bay Lookout: 45 minutes return

  South Bay Lookout: 1¼ hours return

  South Bay: 1¾ hours return

The close proximity of the mountains to the sea makes Kaikoura one of New Zealand's most spectacular locations even without the whale watching, and the open farmland on these walks provides endless views of both coast and peaks. The Kaikoura peninsula was originally an island and was joined to the mainland by debris washed down the Hapuka and Kowhai rivers from the mountains. Once heavily forested, the peninsula was also long occupied by Maori, with at least 11 pa sites identified. Sealers and whalers were attracted to the area early in the nineteenth century, followed by farmers later on.

The seal colony is right by the car park, and you need to keep a sharp eye out as the seals blend easily into the surrounding landscape. Most folk only go up to the first lookout (there is an excellent view of a stepped pa from here), but it is worth continuing on along the cliff-top with views of the mountains to the west, and seals, seabirds and an attractive rocky shoreline below. The car park is sheltered from the southerly wind so be prepared for more exposed conditions on the top.

It is possible to return to the car park along the shore below the cliffs, although this can be tricky at high tide. If this is an appealing option then start the walk around the rocks by the car park as this section of the coast is most affected by the tide. If the tide isn't right and you need to turn back, then you only have to retrace your steps by a matter of a few hundred metres.

A further option is to be dropped off at Point Kean and walk the whole track back to town. From South Bay it is only a 45-minute walk.

Hanmer Forest Park

Forested with a mixture of exotics and natives, it is the imported trees that are the main attraction in the Hanmer region. The forest, originally established in 1903 using prison labour, has extensive plantings of Douglas fir and *Pinus radiata* for timber production, while a number of other species were planted for beautification purposes or to test their suitability for timber.

The forest area is very close to Hanmer Springs village and includes a wide range of good walks, especially attractive in autumn when the deciduous trees are turning colour in the cool mountain climate. And of course the famous hot pools make this a very popular weekend destination.

2 Hanmer Forest Park: Conical Hill   Medium   𝄃   50 minutes return

✳ Mature exotic trees cloak a lookout with fine views over the Hanmer district.

➤ The walk begins at the north end of Conical Hill Road (Hanmer Springs' main street).

A very popular walk on an excellent track, this is a steady uphill climb through mainly conifers, including pine, fir, larch and cypress. From the lookout at the top of the hill (550 m) there are great views of the surrounding mountains and over the township below.

3 Hanmer Forest Park: Woodland Walk
Easy   𝄃   40 minutes return

✳ Deciduous and coniferous woods with the idyllic atmosphere of a bygone age.

➤ From Conical Hill Road, turn right into Jollies Pass Road (to the right just after the information centre) and the walk begins 1 km on the left.

With a totally appropriate name, this walk meanders through a mixture of northern hemisphere deciduous and evergreen trees, and is especially attractive in autumn with the seasonal colour heightened by Hanmer's cool alpine climate. While it does have an attractive wetland with flax, the gentle woodland atmosphere almost makes you expect a Jane Austen heroine to come ambling through at any moment.

4 Hanmer Forest Park: Conical Hill/Woodland Combo

Medium   🚶   1½ hours in total

* Follow up a combination of the previous two walks with a well-earned soak in the springs.

➤ Begin at the north end of Conical Hill Road.

A lack of information boards showing the local tracks is not helpful, especially in a town that completely relies on visitors, but the Majuba Track links the two walks described above. As they are both close to town it is simple to combine them into a longer walk from the village. Start by going up Conical Hill and returning back the same way to the Majuba Track, which intersects the Conical Hill track to the left about halfway down. This joins the Woodland loop track via the wetland. From the Woodland Track exit on Jollies Pass Road, it is only 1 km back to the main street.

Lewis Pass

Much lower than Arthur's Pass, at 864 metres the Lewis Pass is an old Maori greenstone trail that follows the Lewis River south of the pass and the Maruia River to the north. Today the pass is the main route from North Canterbury to the Buller region, though the area does tend to have fewer visitors than many other parts of the South Island. The subalpine vegetation is mainly beech.

5 The Sluice Box   Easy   🚶   15 minutes return

* Where the Maruia River funnels through a narrow gorge.

➤ On SH7, 4.5 km east of Springs Junction, the walk begins from the Marble Hill car park at the beginning of the Lake Daniels walk.

A flat easy walk through mature beech forest to a point where the Maruia River runs clear and deep as it is forced through a narrow gorge of marble. This is an impressive contrast to the broad shallow river by the car park.

6 Waterfall Track   Easy 🚶 20 minutes return

* ✳ Venerable beech forest stands watch over a picture-postcard cascade.
* ➤ On SH7, 9 km east of Springs Junction.

An attractive bush walk through massive ancient beech trees leads to a slender and elegant waterfall that drops 40 metres. Just below the top of the falls the water strikes a rocky ledge and dissipates into a fine spray, before reforming into a more substantial flow lower down.

7 Tarn Walk   Easy 🚶 20 minutes return

* ✳ Moss-covered subalpine beech forest encircles a tranquil mountain tarn.
* ➤ On SH7, 23 km east of Springs Junction.

It is well worth stopping for this well-formed track skirting a small mountain tarn by the car park that, on a still day, is a great place to take a photo of the mountains reflected in the water. From here, the walk loops through stunted alpine beech forest festooned with fine mosses and with views deep into the snowcapped mountains to the north, including Gloriana Peak. There are also excellent identification labels for alpine plants along the track.

8 St Annes Lagoon   Easy 🚶 30 minutes

* ✳ A small pretty lakeshore brimming with birdlife and ideal for a rest stop.
* ➤ On SH1, 3 km north of Cheviot.

A short pleasant walk is to be had beside this small lake packed with birdlife attracted by water in the usually dry North Canterbury region. Planted with lovely deciduous trees, the walk is particularly pretty in autumn or perfect for a shady picnic in summer. This is a good spot to take a break and stretch your legs on the road between Christchurch and Picton.

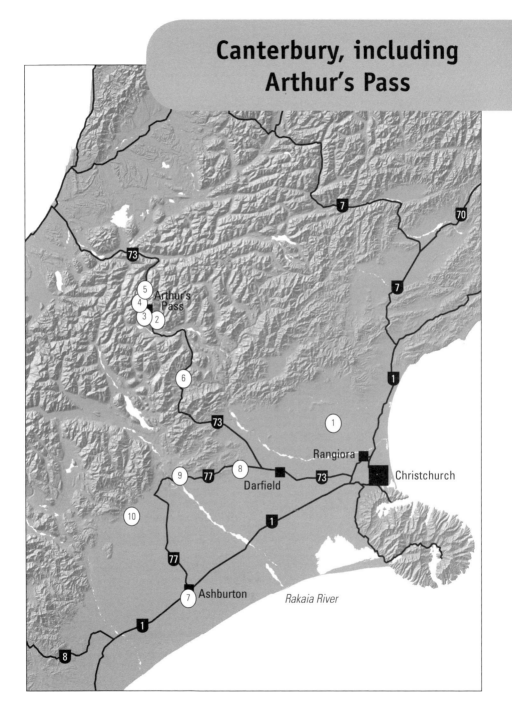

Canterbury, including Arthur's Pass

1 Mt Thomas

✳ The deep lush valleys of this beech forest are alive with the sound of bellbirds.

➤ From Rangiora, take the Lowburn–Glentui Road and Mt Thomas is clearly signposted to the right. The car park is 3 km down the end of this road.

Kereru Track   Easy   🚶   50 minutes return

Both walks start at the main noticeboard, but take note that the signage on the actual tracks can be a bit confusing. This easy loop track, which can be muddy in patches, starts steadily uphill on a well-graded track through handsome beech forest and with the constant accompaniment of the sound of bellbirds.

Wooded Gully/Red Pine Tracks   Medium   🚶   2 hours return

This walk proceeds through handsome beech forest with occasional glimpses of the plains to the east. In addition to bellbirds, keep a sharp eye out for the rare native parrot, the kakariki.

Starting at the main noticeboard, follow the Wooded Gully Track signs uphill. Continue past the junction with the Kereru Track, after which the path becomes steeper and narrower. Eventually you will reach the junction with the Red Pine Track, at which point turn left, heading back downhill until it rejoins the Kereru Track and the return to the car park.

There is also an excellent camping and picnic area at the beginning of these walks with great views over the Canterbury Plains.

Arthur's Pass

The Arthur's Pass area has some of the most dramatic and accessible mountain scenery in the country. The road through the pass traverses two very different climate zones, from the cooler, dry tussocky Canterbury region to the warm and very wet West Coast. Surprising to most people is that Porters Pass in the east, at 942 metres, is slightly higher than Arthur's Pass at 920 metres.

Arthur's Pass village, with its iconic small corrugated-iron huts, is a great base for walks in the Southern Alps, and if you're travelling on the TranzAlpine, you can get off the train here and have plenty of time to do some of them. The following walks can be undertaken in all but the most extreme weather, though the conditions here are notoriously changeable so check at the excellent Department of Conservation information centre if you have any concerns. On these walks you are likely to encounter kea, New Zealand's cheeky and entertaining mountain parrot, so don't leave your belongings too near their prying beaks.

2 Devils Punchbowl   Easy   🚶 50 minutes return

* ✳ A dramatic 131-metre waterfall plunges down a rock face.
* ➤ The track begins on Punchbowl Road off SH73, 600 metres west of the information centre (add 10 minutes if walking from the information centre).

A justifiably popular walk on an excellent track that begins by crossing the footbridge over the Bealey River and then tends on a steady uphill grade through mountain beech, with a flight of wooden steps to the lookout at the end. The viewing platform faces the falls that drop an impressive 131 metres down a sheer cliff face to the rocks below.

Canterbury,
including
Arthur's Pass

3 Bridal Veil Falls   Easy

* ✳ Views of a small picturesque waterfall and the surrounding mountains.
* ➤ The track begins on Punchbowl Road off SH73, 600 metres west of the information centre (add 10 minutes if walking from the information centre).
* 🚶 Lookout: 30 minutes return

  Bridal Veil Track: 1¼ hours return

After crossing the Bealey River footbridge (same as Devils Punchbowl), turn left. This track runs parallel to the main road and leads to a lookout point over the mountains and a distant view of the Bridal Veil Falls. Beyond the lookout the track drops steeply into a gully and then, unfortunately, follows under electricity pylons that are hardly picturesque. The track ends at the main road, and be aware that if you choose to walk back along the road there are no footpaths, parts of the road are very narrow, and cars travel very quickly along here so take care. (In reality, unless you are desperately in need of a walk, the best part of this track is to the lookout and back.)

4 Bealey Valley Easy

✳ A mossy forest floor passage to a tussock clearing with expansive views.

➤ Off SH73, 3 km north of the information centre.

🚶 The Chasm: 20 minutes return

Tussock Clearing: 30 minutes return

The Chasm is a trifle too dramatic a name for this narrow rocky passage on the Bealey River, but it is a very pleasant short walk though moss-carpeted beech forest to a wide clearing with red tussock. There are wide views down through the pass and across to Temple Basin from the clearing.

5 Dobson Nature Walk Easy 🚶 45 minutes return

✳ A close-up view of fascinating alpine vegetation.

➤ Begins off SH73, 3.7 km north of the information centre at either the Temple Basin ski area car park or opposite the Arthur Dobson Memorial at the top of the pass.

From a distance the alpine vegetation on this walk looks rather uniformly dull and uninteresting, but up close the variety and diversity of plant life is astounding. Mountain flax, tussock, turpentine bush and hebe are among the plants that grow here in profusion. Particularly common is the giant Mt Cook lily, which is not a lily but the world's largest buttercup. Recognised by its large round fleshy leaves, it seems too delicate for this harsh mountain climate.

Located at the very top of the pass at 923 metres, this is the most accessible alpine walk on the pass road, and the peak period to see alpine flowers in bloom is from November to February. From the car park, the well-formed track is an easy uphill climb and then loops down to a small wetland alongside Lake Misery and back to the road.

6 Castle Hill/Kura Tawhiti Easy 🚶 Allow 1 hour

✳ Weathered limestone rock formations stand in the open grass country like some fantasy film landscape.

➤ On SH73, 3 km east of Castle Hill, 55 km east of Arthur's Pass.

Although they can be seen from the road, these rocks are just a 10-minute walk away and are worth the trip as they are much more impressive close up than at a distance. Once you reach them there is no set track as such, so you can take as long as you like to stroll around. The rocks themselves have quite a magical feel, and this is a great place to find somewhere perched up high to enjoy the quiet mountain solitude while all around the voices and laughter of the unseen echo mysteriously about the stone formations.

Weathered by years of wear by water and wind, these limestone formations stand in direct contrast to the greywacke rock of the surrounding mountain ranges. It is easy to see why they were also used as a location in the first Narnia film *The Lion, the Witch and the Wardrobe*.

7 Ashburton Domain Easy 🚶 Allow 45 minutes

✳ A large park with something for everyone.

➤ On SH1, opposite the old railway station in Ashburton.

This huge park, a combination of formal gardens, lawns, arboretum and sports fields, is well worth the stop along the long stretch of SH1 between Christchurch and Timaru. Particularly appealing are the magnificent old trees, a mixture of natives and exotics and some well over a century old, of which the conifers are especially impressive. Two small lakes, clearly an old riverbed, add to the appeal and are packed with ducks. In addition to the gardens, there is a children's playground, aviary, skateboard park, plenty of good places for a picnic, and all beautifully maintained. It really is impossible not to stop and take a stroll.

8 Glentunnel Millennium Walk Easy 🚶 1¼ hours

✳ Vestiges of historic potteries, an abandoned train tunnel and an old coal mine.

➤ Starts at the Glentunnel Library, Glentunnel village, SH77.

After first walking around the tiny historic brick library at Glentunnel in order to appreciate the ceramics and the finely crafted brick chimney, continue on up the road past the museum to the old stables that originally housed the pit ponies used in the mine. Just beyond this spot are scattered piles of broken ceramic pipes marking the site of an old pottery.

From here, the walk crosses farmland and in part follows the old Whitecliffs railway, eventually reaching an abandoned rail tunnel built in 1874. Only the entrance is now visible of this tunnel built by the mine owners in order to avoid a 2s 6p per ton toll demanded by the local landowner if the railway crossed his property. The walk ends at the old coal mine closed in 1938 and now blocked, though an old rusting boiler and winch still remain.

9 Rakaia River Gorge Bridges Medium ⅄ 1 hour return

* ✴ Where the wide Rakaia River is forced through a narrow rocky gorge.

* ➤ The walk begins at the car park below the bridge on the north bank of the Rakaia River on SH77.

Part of a longer track on the north bank of the river, the following walk is much shorter with attractive views of the gorge and bridges.

The path is undulating and in most parts sits high above the swirling turquoise water of the river as it squeezes through the narrow gorge. Although the vegetation is sparse, there are many fine old kowhai trees overhanging the water. Eventually the track zigzags up a steep bluff to a wide grassy terrace with an excellent view downriver and over the bridges to the plain beyond. In strong nor'wester winds, large dust storms are created along the broad riverbed.

A ferry service operated at this point until the two bridges linking both banks and Goat Island were built in 1884.

10 Mt Somers/Sharplin Falls Medium ⅄ 1 hour 10 minutes return

* ✴ An attractive forest walk to a small waterfall in a rocky gorge.

* ➤ From Mt Somers on SH72, drive 7 km to Staveley and follow the signposts 4 km to the car park at the end of the road.

The cool beech forest of the Canterbury foothills around Mt Somers and Staveley is in direct contrast to the open plains below and the dry tussock mountain country further inland.

This beautiful forest walk follows the Bowyers Stream to a rocky gorge where the stream splits into two picturesque waterfalls. A short side track along the way leads to the Goldsmith rapids where massive water-sculpted boulders line the stream below a stony bluff and rock slide. Just before the falls, a gantry clinging to a cliff face has good views of the river below and the gorge further upstream.

Part of the track follows the stream bed and involves some rock hopping, though there is an alternative upper-level track if the river is uncomfortably high. This does not add any more time to the walk, is not that much of a climb, and has the added advantage of passing through swathes of crown ferns with occasional glimpses of the plains below.

Christchurch and
Banks Peninsula

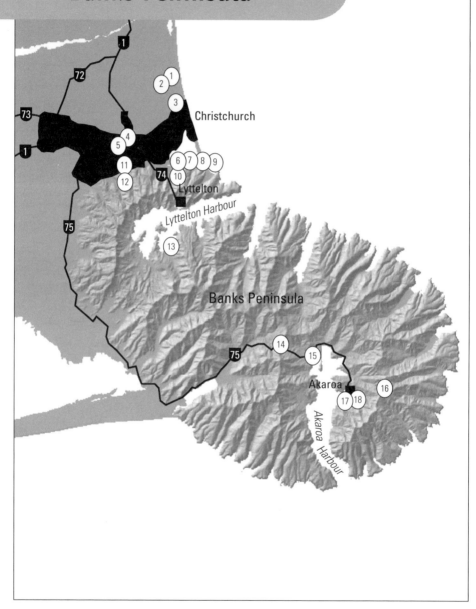

Christchurch City

1 Waimakariri River Mouth   Easy   🚶   Allow 1 hour

✳ A beach, dune and lagoon combination that can be made as long or as short as you like.

➤ The track is in Spencer Park on Heyders Road, which is off Lower Styx Road, north-east of the city. Clearly marked to the left from the beach access that leads from the car park.

The beaches on Pegasus Bay north-east of Christchurch are vast and largely empty even on a hot summer's day (although there is usually a cool wind along this coast), making this a great place for that long lazy beach walk.

It is best to start this walk by strolling north along the beach towards the mouth of the Waimakariri River. When you've had enough of the beach (and the wind), find a track in the dunes, cut directly west and you will meet and turn left on the track that runs along the eastern side of the Brooklands Lagoon from the car park all the way to the river mouth.

If you decide to begin the walk the other way round, your return point on the walk back along the beach is the surf club building (the dunes have a sameness and it is not easy to spot where the return track is otherwise).

2 Brooklands Lagoon   Easy   🚶   30 minutes

✳ A bird-watcher's paradise in a vast salt marsh at the mouth of the Waimakariri River.

➤ The track begins at the information board at the entrance to Spencer Park on Heyders Road, off Lower Styx Road.

Spencer Park is part of a wider complex of parks that encompasses a large area of beach, lagoon, salt marsh and dune country south of the Waimakariri River mouth. Attracting a wide range of wading birds, the area around the Brooklands Lagoon has a number of easy tracks that vary in length. This short sandy loop track is appealing in that it has both a raised viewing platform that gives a good outlook over the tidal flats and a bird hide situated on top of a small dune that is ideal for bird watching. Over 70 bird species have been recorded here including oystercatcher, red-billed gull, spotted shag, white-faced heron, banded dotterel and pied cormorant.

3 Travis Wetland   Easy

✳ Prolific birdlife is the main feature of this unique wetland on the outskirts of Christchurch.

➤ Located in the suburb of Burwood, this wetland has several entrances, but for visitors the best place to start is at the Beach Road entrance, which has information, parking and toilets, and is close to the bird hide.

🚶 Bird hide: 15 minutes return

Loop walk: 1½ hours

A dead flat, well-formed circuit track leads through this large wetland teeming with native and introduced birdlife. Over 50 species have been recorded here, including black swan, shoveler, pukeko, grey duck, mallard, Canada goose and scaup. Thirty-five species of native bird have visited the lagoon, and five species of native duck breed here. In addition to native fauna, at least 60 native plant species are to be found in the wetland.

Considerably modified by human activity over the past 750 years and now encircled by suburban housing, the wetland is gradually being restored with an energetic planting and weed-removal programme. Some of the wetland is still being farmed, however.

From the car park it is a short walk to an excellent bird hide that overlooks a deep pond thronging with birds. Another 20 minutes further on is a tall viewing tower with a wide perspective of the wetland over the treetops. The track then skirts around the edge of the wetland back to the car park. Be aware that cyclists also use this track.

Christchurch and Banks Peninsula

4 Hagley Park and Botanic Gardens   Easy

✳ A marvellous large park of mature trees, sports fields and home to the Christchurch Botanic Gardens.

➤ Rolleston Avenue, Christchurch.

🚶 Hagley Park circuit: 1¾ hours

North Hagley Park circuit: 1 hour

Botanic Gardens: 45 minutes

In 1850, surveyors included in the plan of early Christchurch a park of approximately 202 hectares, and although since reduced in size to 161 hectares, the park today is a mixture of gardens, woodland and sports fields (including the Hagley Golf Club established in 1904). The park is essentially divided in two by Riccarton Avenue, with the southern end being mainly sports fields. In spring the daffodils, bluebells and blossoming cherry trees along Harper Avenue are particularly spectacular. Within the park, the Christchurch Botanic Gardens nestle within a loop of the Avon River, and the formerly swampy area north of the river has been transformed into two small lakes, Victoria and Albert. The complete circuit of the park is 6 km and is popular with joggers.

Covering an area of 30 hectares, the long established Botanic Gardens are reputed to contain more than 10,000 plants. An oak tree planted in July 1863 commemorating the marriage of Prince Albert of Great Britain to Princess Alexandra of Denmark is regarded as the first official planting. Particularly impressive in summer are the fine herbaceous borders well suited to the southern climate, while grouped in the centre of the gardens are the tropical, cactus and orchid houses and a ponga-lined fern house. The elaborate Peacock Fountain, originally erected in 1911 and for many years dismantled and stored due to maintenance problems, was finally restored in 1996. Ornately Edwardian in style and made of cast iron, the fountain was made in the Coalbrookdale foundry in Shropshire, England.

5 Riccarton Bush, Deans Cottage and Riccarton House

Easy 🏃 20 minutes

✳ A small bush remnant and two of Canterbury's most historic houses.

➤ Kahu Road, Riccarton.

Riccarton Bush is a small remnant of the large kahikatea forests once common on the swampy plain around Christchurch. Maori settlers decimated the forests by burning, and European settlers by felling, reducing their once vast extent to mere fragments. Now firmly protected by a predator-free fence, this reserve is too small to sustain much native birdlife, although the vegetation is surprisingly diverse. In addition to kahikatea, the bush also contains totara, rimu, beech, matai and kowhai, and some of the trees may well be over 600 years old.

The Deans family preserved the bush with great foresight, and their cottage is the oldest surviving building on the plain. Built in 1843 to house the newly arrived settlers William and John Deans until resources allowed for a larger dwelling to be constructed, the timber for the cottage came from the bush near the house. Originally the cottage stood closer to the road, and has since been moved to its present site.

Riccarton House, however, is a large and grand Victorian affair, and like many colonial houses was built in several stages over many years as money became available. The first part of the house was completed in 1856, and the last stage, which gives the house its present character, in 1900. Riccarton House now operates as a café and is open every day from 10 am to 4 pm.

6 Barnett Park   Medium 🚶 1½ hours

✳ A lava cave high on the hills with great views over the Heathcote and Avon estuaries.

➤ Barnett Park is well signposted to the right at Moncks Bay on the main road to Sumner, and the track begins at the far end of the playing fields.

This well-formed loop track, with mainly even grades, winds its way up the side of a valley through regenerating bush and past rock bluffs to a flight of 70 wooden steps that leads to a shallow lava cave. From the platform at the entrance to the cave the views to the north are extensive, over the Heathcote and Avon River estuaries, along the coast to the pier at New Brighton and beyond. The track then loops back down the other side of the valley.

Taylors Mistake

Taylors Mistake is famous for the tiny home-built cribs, erected mostly in the 1920s and 1930s, tucked hard into the rock face and in some cases utilising shallow caves and overhangs as part of the structure. In addition to the cribs, Taylors Mistake is also renowned for its lively surf (check out the live webcam: www.taylorssurf.co.nz). At Hobson Bay, just before Taylors Mistake, there is an alternative upper route if high tide prevents walking along the beach.

The origins of the name are somewhat murky, and it is by astounding coincidence that three ships came to grief in this bay all captained by men with the apparently unlucky surname Taylor. Marked on maps as Taylors Mistake as early as 1853, the name finally stuck after the unfortunate American

Captain Taylor grounded his ship the *Volga* here in 1858 after mistaking the bay for the entrance to Lyttelton Harbour.

7 Scarborough to Taylors Mistake

✳ Sweeping prospects atop dramatic sea cliffs around Taylors Mistake.

➤ The walk begins at Nicholson Park on Scarborough Road at Scarborough (located on the left at the top of the road from Sumner to Taylors Mistake).

🚶 Loop walk: Easy, 25 minutes return

Taylors Mistake: Medium, 2 hours return

The short loop walk begins from the car park and leads to the cliff-top with views over Christchurch, Sumner, north to New Brighton and the North Canterbury coast, and east to Taylors Mistake and Godley Head. There is one short steep section with steps.

The Taylors Mistake walk begins from the same car park and follows an undulating path along the top of cliffs that are a sheer drop into the ocean. While there are some short steep sections here too, the track is excellent with seats along the way on which to catch your breath and take in the view. The prospects from this track are to the east and not over Christchurch City.

From the beach, you can either return the way you came or walk up the road, which is quicker and easier, although it only has a footpath part of the way, is narrow in places, and cars belt along it.

8 Taylors Mistake to Godley Head/Boulder Bay   Medium

✳ Open grass and tussock land with sea views in every direction.

➤ The usual starting point is from the car park at Taylors Mistake, but the track is also accessible from the car park at the end of Summit Road.

🚶 Taylors Mistake to Godley Head: 1½ hours one-way

Taylors Mistake to Boulder Bay: 1¾ hours return

This is one of the region's most popular walks. An excellent wide track winds along the coast through open grass and tussock land passing the tiny cribs at Boulder Bay and with views all along the way (white flipper penguins have been reintroduced to the area around Boulder Bay). The track then gradually rises from the rocky shore to Godley Head.

The views from the headland rising 120 metres out of the sea are superb, to the north over Pegasus Bay and south over the entrance to Lyttelton harbour. A lighthouse was built here as early as 1865, and in 1939 a substantial coastal battery was established to protect the harbour. At one point, 400 men and women were stationed here and today three gun emplacements and several other military buildings still remain.

Be aware that mountain bikers also use these tracks and can take them very fast, especially downhill.

Port Hills

9 Godley Head Tunnel   Medium ⅄ 40 minutes return

* World War II gun emplacements and a 120-metre tunnel.

➤ From the city, take Evans Pass Road from Sumner up to the Summit Road, then turn left and continue to the car park at the very end.

From the Godley Head car park, a short and well-graded track zigzags down a steep hillside to Mechanics Bay and World War II gun emplacements. Especially appealing is a 120-metre access tunnel right at sea level.

10 Bridle Path

* The original track from Lyttelton to Heathcote with great views over the city and Lyttelton Harbour.

➤ The Christchurch end of the track begins at Bridle Path Road, Heathcote.

⅄ Heathcote to Lyttelton: Hard, 1½ hours one-way

Heathcote to the Summit: Hard, 2 hours return

Summit to Heathcote: Medium, 40 minutes one-way

In 1851 this track was the main access from Lyttelton to the fledgling settlement of Christchurch, and for the early settlers laden with baggage this trip must have been a very daunting introduction to their new home. It is easy to see why the Lyttelton rail tunnel, opened in 1867, was such a priority if the tiny settlement was to flourish. A monument commemorating the endurance of pioneer women can be found on the summit, and even today the Bridle Path is still a challenging walk.

The track is now a 4WD road, and while well formed, the uphill trudge from either side is a good workout. The views from the summit over both Christchurch and Lyttelton are superb, and you do get a little appreciation of the pioneering spirit even with modern clothing and a light backpack. An alternative to walking the uphill track is to take the gondola to the top and walk back down to either the Heathcote Valley or Lyttelton where the track ends near the southern entrance to the road tunnel. Even walking downhill you will still need good footwear as the track has small loose stones that can be surprisingly slippery!

11 Victoria Park, Harry Ell Track   Medium 人 2 hours return

✱ Bush and formal planting mix in this large park on the hills above Cashmere.

➤ The walk starts at the Sign of the Takahe, Dyers Pass Road, Cashmere.

While its name celebrates Queen Victoria's Golden Jubilee in 1897, this park was first established as early as 1870 with formal planting under way in the 1880s. Now covering over 260 hectares, Victoria Park is planted in a wide variety of both native and exotic trees and is a maze of walking and mountain bike tracks.

A local Member of Parliament, Harry Ell, envisioned a series of rest houses linked by walking tracks along the summit of the Port Hills above Christchurch. Originally the rest houses were to offer both accommodation and meals, but only the Tudor/Gothic 'Sign of the Takahe' was ever completed to the scale projected. Harry died in 1934, and in addition to the Sign of the Takahe (finally completed in 1949), also built were the more modest Sign of the Kiwi, Sign of the Bellbird and Sign of the Packhorse.

Victoria Park was also the scene of one of New Zealand's most famous murders when, on 22 June 1954, Pauline Parker aged 16 and Juliet Hulme aged 15 bashed Pauline's mother to death with a brick. Peter Jackson later turned this tragic story into the film *Heavenly Creatures*.

The Harry Ell Track begins at the Sign of the Takahe, and is an excellent well-graded walkway that leads mainly through regenerating bush, all the way up to the Sign of the Kiwi at the top of Dyers Pass Road. The track parallels the road and unfortunately the traffic noise can be a bit off-putting at times. To avoid backtracking, an alternative is to take the Thomson and Latters Spur tracks back to the start. These tracks can be confusing, but if you just continue to walk downhill you won't go too far wrong.

Be aware that mountain bikers also use some of these tracks, though the Harry Ell Track is for walkers only.

12 Crater Rim Walkway

No one seems quite able to agree where this walk begins or ends. Some have it starting at the Sign of the Takahe and going through to Cooper's Knob, while others insist it starts at Godley Head and ends at the bottom of the Rapaki Track. Either way, this lengthy track runs along the ridge of the old crater that is Lyttelton Harbour, and despite the rocky and rugged nature of the landscape, the following three short walks are relatively easy. Bush remnants are a reminder that the peninsula was once heavily forested.

Mt Sugar Loaf   Medium   ⅄   50 minutes return

* Superb views over the entire peninsula, Christchurch City and the Canterbury Plains.

➤ Starts opposite the Sign of the Kiwi at the top of Dyers Pass Road.

Easily recognised by the 120-metre high transmitter on top of Mt Sugar Loaf, this loop walk begins up the easy grade of the Cedric Track leading to a car park below the transmitter, and then follows the sealed road to the summit with amazing views over Banks Peninsula, Christchurch City, the Canterbury Plains and the Southern Alps beyond.

From the top, walk down the eastern slope through the tussock to the stile, which is visible from the summit. While there is no track as such, the tussock is short so you won't get lost. Immediately over the stile, take the track to the right, which meanders through regenerating bush back to the car park.

Kennedy Bush/Sign of the Bellbird   Medium   ⚚   Up to 1 hour

- ✸ One of the few native bush remnants on the Banks Peninsula.

- ➤ On the Summit Road, 4.8 km from the Sign of the Kiwi at the top of Dyers Pass Road.

Mainly consisting of mahoe with some totara and kowhai, this small bush remnant is a reminder that the entire peninsula was once densely covered with native forest. The signage for the walk is a bit confusing, but start to the left of the rock shelter that is the Sign of the Bellbird and continue downhill through the bush. When you've had enough (remember it's uphill all the way back), take one of the tracks to the right that will lead back uphill to the shelter. It is a small reserve so you won't get lost.

There is a superb view of Lyttelton Harbour across the road from the beginning of the walk.

Gibraltar Rock   Medium   ⚚   40 minutes return

- ✸ Excellent views over the Canterbury Plains from a high rocky outcrop.

- ➤ On the Summit Road, 9 km from the Sign of the Kiwi at the top of Dyers Pass Road.

The walk starts through a small patch of regenerating bush and then over tussocked farmland to an outcrop of volcanic rock with great views over the city, plains and south to Lake Ellesmere. The walk is easy to the outcrop, but the less nimble might find the final scramble to the top a bit of a challenge.

13 Orton Bradley Park, Big Rock Walk

Medium   ⚚   40 minutes return

- ✸ A pleasant walk to good views from atop a gigantic rock.

- ➤ Clearly signposted on the right at Charteris Bay, 5 km from Diamond Harbour on the south side of Lyttelton Harbour. There is an entrance fee to the park.

Orton Bradley Park centres on the historic buildings of a farm established by Canterbury pioneer Orton Bradley, and the stone shepherd's cottage built in 1848 is the oldest building of its type in the region. The rhododendron collection is one of the most extensive in the country and the best time to see the flowers is in spring, when most of the blooms are at their peak.

The Big Rock walk follows a pretty stream through exotic trees of mainly poplar, birch and eucalypt, and is an easy trek until you reach the rock. It then becomes a steep climb to the base of the rock and then a final, but not too difficult, scramble to the top. From this lofty perch there are views down the valley to the harbour and high into the hills towards Mt Herbert.

Akaroa Harbour

Both Akaroa and Lyttelton Harbours are old volcanoes and now form magnificent deep waterways, surrounded by rugged steep hills, tiny bays and beaches. Today only fragments of bush remain.

14 Montgomery Park Scenic Reserve Easy ⋏ 10 minutes return

* ✳ A gnarled 2000-year-old totara tree looking every bit its age.

* ➤ From Hilltop on the Akaroa Road, turn left into Summit Road and the reserve is on the left, 500 metres from the intersection.

A short steep walk leads up through bush to an ancient totara tree believed to be at least 2000 years old. While not a particular large specimen (it has a girth of 8 metres), it is rather battered and certainly looks its age. This ancient tree is a poignant reminder that the peninsula, now largely grass and tussock, was once thickly forested and alive with birdsong.

15 Onawe Peninsula Easy ⋏ 1 hour return

* ✳ Historical pa site on a teardrop-shaped peninsula with great views over the harbour.

* ➤ At Barry's Bay turn into Onawe Flat Road, and the walk starts from the car park at the end.

Onawe Peninsula, shaped like a giant teardrop, juts out into the waters of the upper Akaroa Harbour and rises to a height of over 100 metres. Linked to the mainland by a narrow strip of land and virtually cut off at high tide, this was an ideal position for a fortified pa. In 1832, on his conquest of the South Island, Ngati Toa chief Te Rauparaha had trouble taking the pa and in the end used local captives to trick his way in, culminating in a terrible massacre of the inhabitants followed by a cannibal feast at Barrys Bay.

The track starts to the right of the car park and skirts along the beach (not over the bluff) and is difficult right on high tide. From there it is an easy walk through open grassland to the top, though today the outlines of the pa are hard to discern.

16 Ellangowan Scenic Reserve   Medium 🚶 45 minutes return

* ✱ Superb views over the whole peninsula from a tussocky hilltop.

* ➤ On the road from Duvauchelle, 3 km north of Akaroa turn right into Long Bay Road. At the top of this hill at the intersection of Summit and Long Bay Roads, take the metalled road off to the left (Hickory Bay Road) and the reserve is marked 1 km on the left.

From this high rocky bluff there are spectacular views over the entire peninsula, while to the west lie the Southern Alps and Pegasus Bay far to the north. It is not a hard climb, although the track varies from rough to non-existent and the top can be very exposed and windy. It is easy to lose the track, but as the vegetation is open and only waist-high it is impossible to get lost. You will also need to wear long trousers as the stunted gorse and wild Spaniard can be nasty on bare legs.

Akaroa

In 1838, Captain Langlois, a French sea captain who had earlier visited Akaroa, established the Nanto-Bordelaise Company, and in 1840 set sail for New Zealand with a small contingent of French and German families with the intention of establishing a French colony. By the time they arrived in August 1840 on the ship *Comte de Paris*, the Treaty of Waitangi had been signed, and the French found themselves in what was now a British colony. Not wishing to return, the French and German emigrants established themselves around Akaroa Harbour and were later to be joined by British settlers.

The town has numerous historic buildings all within a short walking distance, and the Rue Jolie and Rue Balguerie are particularly notable for their historic cottages. One of the oldest buildings in Canterbury, the two-roomed Langlois Eteveneaux cottage, was built between 1841 and 1846 for Aimable Langlois, the brother of Captain Langlois, in a distinctly French style.

The following two short walks are within easy walking distance of the town, though both at the time of writing were poorly maintained.

17 L'Aube Hill/French Cemetery   Easy ⅄ 20 minutes return

* ✳ The oldest cemetery in Canterbury.

* ➤ The walk begins in the Rue Lavaud on the corner of Rue Pompallier and Rue Brittan, Akaroa.

This is the site of the old French cemetery established in 1842 and the oldest in the region. The cemetery was originally surrounded by weeping willows said to have come from a cutting of a tree on Napoleon's grave in St Helena. The cemetery fell into disrepair and in 1926 a simple monument was erected on the site. The walk leads uphill from the town through regenerating bush.

18 Stanley Park   Medium ⅄ 30 minutes return

* ✳ Regenerating bush leads to unimpeded views of Akaroa Harbour.

* ➤ Starts to the left of the fire station on Beach Road, Akaroa.

This loop walk is a bit rough and not well signposted, but is a pleasant outing from the town with views of the harbour. In the bushy areas keep an eye out for unusual jet-black fantails.

Just after starting the walk you quickly reach a grassy area. Take the track to the right over the stile and walk uphill through regenerating bush to another large open area from where there are good views over Akaroa Harbour. From here, follow the fence-line to the right, taking the track downhill to Walnut Avenue and via Rue Jolie back to the Beach Road start point.

South Canterbury, Mackenzie Country and Mt Cook

Peel Forest Park

Covering over 700 hectares on the southern bank of the Rangitata River in the foothills of the Southern Alps, Peel Forest Park is a remnant of a much larger forest burnt by early Maori and milled by Pakeha settlers. The climate at Mt Peel is distinct from that of both the plains and the high country further inland. With a much higher rainfall supporting a rich and diverse flora and fauna, this forest is home to a large number of native birds and trees including giant totara, matai and kahikatea. The variety of ferns is especially surprising, and a third of all native fern types can be found here.

The park has a wide range of walking tracks, and jet-boat and rafting companies provide trips through the Rangitata Gorge. The walking tracks start at two main areas, Blandswood and Te Wanahu Flat, both clearly signposted and within 2 km of Mt Peel village.

1 Peel Forest Park: Dennistoun Bush   Easy   45 minutes return

✳ Mature native forest and relics of a sawmilling past.

➤ From Mt Peel village, take the Blandswood Road and the walk begins 1.7 km down this road on the left.

Massive totara, matai and kahikatea feature on the flat loop walk through Dennistoun Bush. There is a short detour to an old sawpit, testament to the extensive milling operations in the area during the late nineteenth and early twentieth centuries.

2 Peel Forest Park: Big Tree Walk   Easy   30 minutes return

✳ Enormous thousand-year-old totara, lord of its native bush surrounds.

➤ The track begins from the Te Wanahu Flat car park, which has toilets and a shelter, 2 km from Mt Peel village.

An easy stroll through dense native bush to a massive totara standing 31 metres high with a girth of 8.5 metres and estimated to be at least a thousand years old.

3 Peel Forest Park: Acland Falls   Medium   🚶 1 hour 20 minutes

✳ A pretty waterfall set deep in lush bush.

➤ Begins from the Te Wanahu Flat car park, 2 km from Mt Peel village.

From the car park, take the Allans Track that leads steadily uphill on a path that can be muddy in places. Just before the waterfall the track drops down to a creek, and this last short section along the creek bed is a bit rough and slippery. The 14-metre waterfall is more like a waterslide and drops gently down a mossy rock face into a shallow pool. On the return trip, take the Acland Track that leads straight downhill to the road, from where it is a quick 500-metre stretch back to the car park.

Mt John/Mackenzie Country

Rising above the icy waters of Lake Tekapo, Mt John is famous for ultra-clear night skies, especially in winter, and the University of Canterbury operates an astronomical observatory on the summit (tours arranged through Earth and Sky: www.earthandsky.co.nz). Sitting isolated from other hills, the views from the top are unsurpassed and encompass the whole Mackenzie Basin, Lake Tekapo, Lake Alexandrina, tiny Lake McGregor, the headwaters of the Godley River, and the Southern Alps. At over 1000 metres altitude, the climate is definitely alpine. While the heights can be very exposed and extremely windy, the rainfall is low, sunshine hours are high, and in summer it can become a very hot climb to the top.

South Canterbury, Mackenzie Country and Mt Cook

4 Mt John Summit   Medium   🚶 2 hours return

✳ Magnificent views over Lake Tekapo and the Mackenzie Country.

➤ From SH8 at Tekapo, turn down to the lake on Lakeside Drive and towards the camping ground. The track begins to the right of the ice-skating rink at the end of the road through the camping ground.

Setting off from the lake edge, the well-formed path is a steady, rather than steep, walk to the summit. Initially the track is through larch, but once clear of the tree line the terrain is open tussock. Just beyond this point the Summit

Track meets the Circuit Track, but continue straight ahead as this is the easiest uphill grade to the top, where there is a smart café and the observatory buildings.

On the return trip, drop down to the Circuit Track below the café and turn left. This takes you around to an excellent information board and magnificent views of Lake Tekapo, the Southern Alps and the Mackenzie Basin. From there, continue the circuit around the summit to the left until you rejoin the Summit Track, from where you return downhill to the start.

5 Mt John Circuit Easy 🚶 40 minutes return

✸ Endless views of the Mackenzie Country from this tussock-lined track.

➤ From Tekapo township, head towards Mt Cook on SH8. Just west of the township the road to Mt John turns off to the right. The road to the summit is sealed.

This track starts at the summit of Mt John, and is a worthwhile walk if you have driven to the top. After a short downhill walk from the café, turn right at the Circuit Track and continue around the summit anticlockwise. This way you avoid a steep uphill section. The track meanders around the summit through deep tussock and includes the excellent information board that details all the natural landmarks. The views are unrelenting.

Aoraki/Mt Cook

New Zealand's highest mountain at 3754 metres, and known in Maori as Aoraki or 'the sky piercer', sits at the head of a dramatic glacial valley. The mountain is at the heart of the Mt Cook National Park, covering more than 70,000 hectares and containing all but one of New Zealand's peaks reaching over 3000 metres. The area is a magnet for serious mountain climbers, though not one to be treated lightly as the mountain has taken numerous lives. The first successful ascent was on Christmas Day 1894. The Department of Conservation office has excellent displays on the natural and human history of the area and up-to-date information on weather and track conditions.

6 Aoraki/Mt Cook: Kea Point   Easy   🚶 1 hour return

✴ A panoramic lookout over the Mueller Glacier and deep within the mountains of the Southern Alps.

➤ Just before Mt Cook village, turn right into Hooker Valley Road and drive to the Whitehorse Hill camping ground car park at the end. The track starts from here.

Meandering through matagouri and mountain totara, this walk skirts the debris of the Mueller Glacier on its way to a spectacular lookout point in an alpine basin surrounded by mountains. Below the lookout is the terminal of the Mueller Glacier, not white and pristine but strewn with gravel. The glacier lake lies deep within crumbling moraine cliffs and contains mighty blocks of slowly melting ice.

While graceful Aoraki at the end of the Hooker Valley dominates the scene, Mt Sefton looms high above the Mueller Glacier with the Huddleston Glacier clinging to its rocky flanks. The return trip offers great views back down the glacier-carved Tasman Valley.

7 Aoraki/Mt Cook: Governors Bush   Medium   🚶 50 minutes

✴ A rare patch of bush with native birds and a good lookout vantage.

➤ 750 metres from the information centre on the Mt Cook village loop road.

The dark-green swathe of Governors Bush climbing the slopes behind Mt Cook village is the only bush in the area and is the best place to see native birds or walk when the weather isn't so good. The track begins by a large trampers' shelter and tends steadily uphill through silver beech to a lookout point over the valley and towards Aoraki in the distance. From there the track drops down and joins the Red Tarns Track which leads back to the road, from where it is a short step back to the car park. In the bush keep an eye out for tomtit, tui, bellbird and fantail.

8 Tasman Glacier and Blue Lakes   Medium

☀ New Zealand's longest glacier lies in the shadow of Aoraki/Mt Cook.

➤ Just before Mt Cook village, turn right into Tasman Valley Road and continue 8 km to the car park. The road is gravel but in good condition.

🚶 Lookout: 40 minutes return

Blue Lakes: Add 10 minutes

Tasman Lake: Add 30 minutes

With Aoraki stealing the show, it is easy to overlook the Tasman Glacier, which at 30 km is the longest glacier in the country and reaches far into the mountains. The main track from the car park is a steady uphill with steps and a short rocky scramble to the top at the end. The lookout point is atop a hill of debris overlooking a vast landscape of rock and ice torn apart by the glacier. However, don't come expecting shimmering blue ice as the glacier has been steadily shrinking over the past 100 years, leaving a thick layer of rocks and gravel covering the ice. While the Tasman Glacier resembles a quarry, the ice is much deeper than it looks, and goes down over 100 metres. From the lookout, Aoraki is visible to the left.

The Blue Lakes, these days a distinctly green colour, are visible from the track, and for a closer look there is a short side track leading down to them – but watch out for the prickly wild Spaniard! Likewise, a side track leads to the terminal lake of the glacier with huge blocks of melting ice drifting ponderously in the icy green water.

9 Clay Cliffs   Medium   🚶 Allow 50 minutes

☀ Dramatic 'badlands' landscape in a high-country setting.

➤ 4 km north of Omarama, turn left into Quailburn Road, and after 4 km turn into Henburn Road. The gate is another 4 km along this road, and from there it is yet another 4 km to the car park. The cliffs are on private land and there is a small entrance fee.

The Clay Cliffs are an unusual example of a 'badlands' landscape formed over many thousands of years by water eroding the soft gravelly soils to create deep gullies and tall pillar-like formations known as 'hoodoos'. These unusual natural structures are formed when rock protects the soil from rain and prevents the soft gravels beneath from eroding, creating high fluted configurations.

While you can walk along the 4WD track along the bottom of the cliff, it is worth exploring into the formations themselves, though these side tracks are pretty rough and involve pushing your way through briar and matagouri.

10 Kakahu Escarpment Easy 人 30 minutes return

✳ A smooth wall of rock soars above surrounding farmland.

➤ The walk begins on Hall Road, off the Winchester Hanging Rock Road, 15 km from Geraldine via Hilton. The walk begins 200 metres from the lime kiln by the bridge.

A short walk across farmland, which can be muddy in places when wet, leads to a magnificent wave of rock sculpted by the elements and rising dramatically above its environs. Huge weathered mushroom-shaped boulders lie at the base of the escarpment. Take a little extra time to visit the historic and well-preserved lime kiln built in 1876, a few hundred metres down the road.

11 Opihi Rock Art Easy 人 1½ hours return

✳ One of the most important pieces of rock art in New Zealand.

➤ Opihi Vineyard, 804 Opihi Road, Hanging Rock (off SH8 from Pleasant Point), South Canterbury.

Beginning at the Opihi Vineyard Café, this walk crosses private farmland to one of the most significant and more accessible pieces of Maori rock art in the country. Located in a rock overhang, the 2-metre-long taniwha is unique in that it is so large and so distinct (much rock art is hard to access and difficult to see). Highly stylised and surprisingly modern, this specimen was featured on the New Zealand two-shilling stamp introduced in the 1960s.

Note that you must first obtain permission to view this art and directions from the café located in the historic 1882 homestead, which is open seven days a week from 11 am to 5 pm. Combining the best of both worlds, reward yourself with a glass of wine and some good food after your exertions.

South Canterbury, Mackenzie Country and Mt Cook

Timaru

12 Dashing Rocks   Easy   𝗑   30 minutes

✳ A great coastal walk that includes a small rock arch.

➤ The track begins at the corner of Pacific and Westcote streets, Timaru.

This loop walk follows a coastal bluff just north of Caroline Bay. It was once a coastal whaling lookout, with wide views back to the city over Waimataitai Beach and along the coast. The two impressive rock arches collapsed recently in a storm, but equally attractive are the geometric patterns in the old lava flows from distant Mt Horrible that underlie the clay.

The beginning of the track on the corner of Pacific and Westcote Streets is just below the road and the sign is a bit hard to see, while the smell of the nearby freezing works can at times be a bit off putting. For those wanting a longer walk there is a track from Caroline Bay and along Waimataitai Beach to Dashing Rocks.

13 Caroline Bay   Easy   𝗑   45 minutes

✳ A popular seaside resort with a strong Edwardian flavour.

➤ You can begin the walk from the car park off Evans Street or walk down the Piazza steps from Stafford Street, Timaru.

The development of the breakwater in 1890 caused an alteration in sea currents and led to Caroline Bay becoming a broad sandy beach. In 1911 an association was formed to develop a resort along European lines and it was that year that the first Caroline Bay Carnival was held. Nearly 100 years later, the carnival is still going strong. Above the bay, the Hydro Grand Hotel is reminiscent of the seaside establishments of Britain.

Today the area is a mix of historic buildings, gardens, a children's playground, a skateboard park and a walk through an aviary, while the Piazza above the bay has become a popular café strip. Starting either from the car park or from the bottom of the steps, the walk is a pleasant loop that takes in all the main attractions including Bay Hall, a dance hall built in 1923; the walk through the bird aviary; the 1932 Bay Tearooms; the Soundshell; the Willow Walk formed in 1903; and a try-pot used by whalers based in the bay between 1839 and 1840.

14 Timaru Botanic Gardens Easy ⅄ 30 minutes

✳ Surprisingly large gardens with a touch of Edwardian grandeur.

➤ Corner of King and Queen Streets, Timaru.

Tucked away just south of the city centre, these gardens are much larger than they appear from the main road. Established in 1864, they are a fine example of Victorian and Edwardian garden styles. In addition to the formal flowerbeds there is an aviary, fern house, rose gardens and a rhododendron and azalea collection; plus the very grand Cenotaph War Memorial is also located within the grounds. The species rose collection is the largest of its type in New Zealand.

The former tea kiosk is delightfully remembered as 'Erected in 1923 by the Floral Fete Committee', while the band rotunda was built in 1911 to celebrate the Coronation of George V and Queen Mary. Completing the attractions is a statue to the Scots poet Robbie Burns and the Queen Victoria Sunken Gardens.

15 South Beach Easy ⅄ 1 hour return

✳ An exposed shingle beach, coastal wetland and formal gardens excursion.

➤ Patiti Point Reserve, end of South Street, Timaru.

This loop walk begins near the Caledonian Grounds at Patiti Point where there are good views along the exposed coast and the old iron anchor of a sailing ship. Head south along the broad shingle beach (South Beach is not suitable for swimming), and then turn right into the Saltwater Creek walkway, an area of marsh currently undergoing restoration with native trees, sedges and other salt-tolerant plants. The track sits above the creek and marshy lake giving a good view of the numerous wading and migratory birds that make this reserve their home.

Return via King Street (SH1), then turn right into James Street and detour through the Botanic Gardens and the historic Timaru Cemetery back to Patiti Point.

South Canterbury, Mackenzie Country and Mt Cook

16 Kelcey's Bush Easy 🚶 30 minutes return

✳ A small elegant waterfall in a rare vestige of bush.

➤ At the end of Mill Road, 8 km from Queen Street, Waimate (the main street).

Kelcey's Bush is a small bush remnant of the extensive forests that once blanketed the Hunters Hills. The forest was destroyed in a disastrous fire that swept the hills in 1878 and burnt down 70 homes as well as a Maori settlement, and permanently ruined the flourishing timber industry. The Hunters Hills are also home to Bennett's wallaby, a native of south-eastern Australia that was released here in 1875 to foster a fur industry. Now considered a pest, it is much sought after by hunters, and for an up-close view there is a wallaby enclosure in Victoria Park in town.

This short easy walk leads through beautiful old tree fuchsias to the modest but pretty Sanders Falls. Tree fuchsias are the largest fuchsia in the world and one of only two deciduous native trees.

South Canterbury,
Mackenzie Country
and Mt Cook

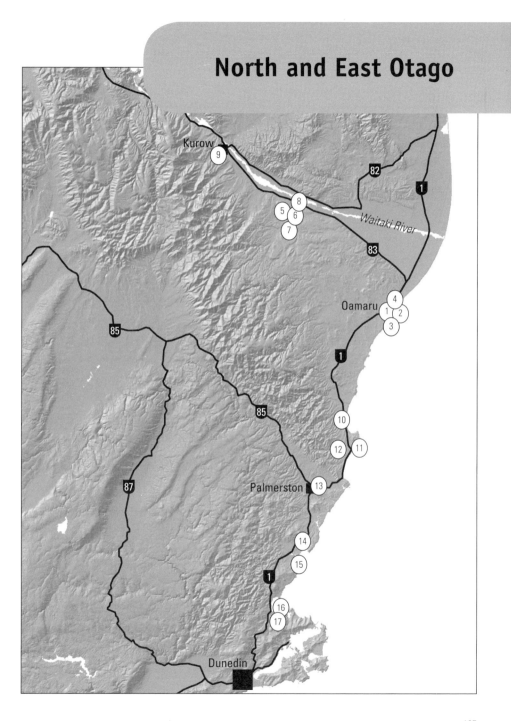

North and East Otago

Oamaru

Naturally sheltered from the worst of the southerly weather by Cape Wanbrow, Oamaru attracted early settlement by Maori and was also home to sealers and whalers in the first half of the nineteenth century. With the construction of the breakwater beginning in 1871, Oamaru quickly became an important port town – especially after the development of refrigerated export meat shipments in 1884 – and the picturesque harbour now shelters a small fishing fleet. The rocks for the breakwater came from the quarry that is now home to the blue penguin colony.

1 Historic Thames and Harbour Streets

Easy   入   Allow 1 hour return

✳ Stunning Victorian heritage buildings built of Oamaru stone.

➤ Begin at the junction of Thames and Severn streets.

Oamaru has without a doubt the finest collection of Victorian buildings in New Zealand and the grandest of these are situated along a short section of Thames Street. Most were built in the short period between 1870 and 1885 when the town flourished as an important port. Eventually, improved rail links replaced the port as a hub of transport and the town became a quiet backwater. The lack of any major development through the twentieth century no doubt saved these fine buildings. What also makes Oamaru unique is that local stone was for the most part the exclusive construction material, giving the town a uniform look unusual in this country.

The historic buildings are mainly in two areas and within easy walking distance of each other. The grander edifices are located on Thames Street (part of which is SH1) and include the Bank of New South Wales (1883, and now the Forrester Gallery), National Bank (1871), St Luke's Anglican Church (1876), first Post Office (1864, and now a restaurant), Post Office (1883, and now the Waitaki Council offices), Courthouse (1882), Opera House (1907) and Athenaeum (1882, now housing the North Otago Museum).

At the southern end of Thames Street turn left into Itchen Street (the information centre is on the corner of Thames and Itchen streets) and then walk straight ahead into Harbour Street. The working area for the port, Harbour Street is totally Victorian in character and has an appealing, intimate feel.

The buildings here started off as warehouses, port offices and grain stores, in contrast to their more distinguished relatives on Thames Street, and today house galleries and craft shops as well as, tucked down a side alley, the famous Penguin Club, with a reputation as one of the best music venues in the country (www.thepenguinclub.co.nz). Significant buildings include Smith's Grain Store (1881), the Union Bank (1878), Customs House (1882), NZ Loan and Mercantile Warehouse (1882) and the Harbour Board Office (1876). A good place to finish your walk is the Criterion Hotel in Tyne Street. Built in 1877, the pub was closed in 1906 when Oamaru went 'dry', and only reopened in 1998.

At the end of Harbour Street turn right into Tyne Street and back to Thames Street, though at this point you might like to continue walking around to the harbour and breakwater, which will add another 40 minutes to your tour.

2 Graves Walkway   Easy   🚶   30 minutes

* Historic vantage point on Oamaru via a penguin colony and ancient lava flows.

➤ The walk begins at the end of Waterfront Road by the blue penguin colony.

The smallest of all the penguins, the blue penguin is common throughout New Zealand and Australia, but Oamaru is the only place where the numbers are reasonably large and the birds easy to see as they make their way at dusk from the sea to nests in the old quarry. The colony itself was only established relatively recently with just 33 breeding pairs in 1992, but now numbers over 120 pairs.

The visitors' centre at the colony has superb information on both the penguins and the natural history of the area, with a special observation stand offering an excellent yet undisturbed view of the birds. There is an entry fee to the stand, which opens for viewing just before sundown when the birds come ashore for the night. Numbers vary considerably depending on the time of year, so check when buying tickets as to how many penguins are likely to come ashore that evening.

Accessed through the blue penguin colony, this walk follows the coast around old lava flows to Cape Wanbrow, but does not now go all the way to Bushy Beach. To extend the walk you can take the steeper return path up to the historic lookout point above Oamaru with excellent views over the town and port. Return to the town via Tamar and Tyne streets.

North and East Otago

3 Bushy Beach Yellow-eyed Penguin Colony

Easy   𝄈   20 minutes return

* ✳ A hide set above this beach is an ideal spot to observe one of the world's rarest penguins.

* ➤ From the centre of Oamaru, take Tyne Street, which becomes Bushy Beach Road, and go to the car park at the very end.

A small colony of rare yellow-eyed penguins has established itself at Bushy Beach just south of Oamaru. The hoiho or yellow-eyed penguin is considerably larger than the blue and much less sociable, preferring nesting spots isolated from other avian neighbours. Yellow-eyed penguins come ashore earlier in the day than the blue penguin and the best time to see them is late afternoon. Because they are more sensitive to human disturbance, the beach is closed after 3 pm, and a small hide sited in the bushes above is an easy walk from the car park.

4 Skyline Walkway, Oamaru   Easy   𝄈   1½ hours

* ✳ A popular circuit with views over Oamaru takes in a variety of local features.

* ➤ The walk begins off Chelmer Street near the main car park at the Oamaru Public Gardens off SH1, Oamaru.

This varied loop walk begins from the Public Gardens (worth a visit in their own right) where you cross over Chelmer Street to Chess Street, a short steep street with the track beginning to your left (and oddly enough not signposted). From Chess Street, the track heads uphill on the only steep part of the walk. In open farmland at the top is an unusual collection of eucalypts that will gladden any Aussie's heart. From there the track leads to the small local observatory, but just before this turn right and cross Eden Street to take a short detour up the hill to the walk's best views, which overlook Oamaru, the port and Cape Wanbrow. Then head back downhill through the pine forest and Glen Warren to Eden Street. Walk down Eden Street and turn right into Reed Street, which leads back to the gardens. If you have the time, visit the Janet Frame House at 56 Eden Street, where one of New Zealand's most influential authors spent her childhood.

Duntroon/Waitaki Valley

North Otago features some of New Zealand's most interesting geology, and the area around Duntroon (on SH83, west of Oamaru) contains some fascinating rock formations and fossils that are easily accessible from the road. The Vanished World Centre in Duntroon is an excellent starting point to brush up on your geology, with a collection of impressive fossils up to 30 million years old, including prehistoric penguins, whales and dolphins and some species that are still to be classified. There is a small entrance fee (www.vanishedworld.co.nz).

North Otago and South Canterbury are also home to numerous Maori rock art sites, though many of them are rudimentary and difficult to reach. However, at Duntroon there are two sites that are accessible and where the art is vivid and easy to discern.

A short loop drive from Duntroon covers the following four walks and will take around 2 hours including walking.

5 Earthquakes   Easy

✳ Explore a dinosaur bone-yard on an ancient seabed.

➤ From Duntroon village, turn off SH83 by the church onto Earthquake Road. The walk begins 6.5 km down this road on the left.

🚶 To the whale fossil: 10 minutes return
For the valley: 40 minutes return

At Earthquakes huge rocks have broken away from the cliffs to expose fossils on an ancient seabed. The highlight is a well-preserved whale fossil from the late Oligocene period, approximately 23–28 million years ago. From the whale, the track wanders in and around huge boulders weathered over time and a rich source of fossils, but take care as rocks are still prone to fall here and there are sudden drops and crevasses concealed in the long grass. While the area is called Earthquakes, the exposed cliff face was actually the result of a massive landslide.

6 Elephant Rocks   Easy   🚶   Allow 30 minutes return

- ✳ Primordial limestone rocks litter a fantasy-film landscape.
- ➤ 6 km from Duntroon on Island Cliff Road, off Livingstone–Duntroon Road.

Dating from the Oligocene period and subsequently shaped by water and wind, these huge weathered limestone rocks take their name from both their grey colouring and their general elephantine shape. What makes this landscape particularly appealing is that the rocks stand clear and stark amid the short grass. Parts of *The Lion, the Witch and the Wardrobe* were shot here.

7 Anatini Whale Fossil   Easy

- ✳ An excellent fossil specimen protected from the elements.
- ➤ 7 km from Duntroon on Island Cliff Road, off the Livingstone–Duntroon Road (1 km from Elephant Rocks).
- 🚶 To the whale fossil: 10 minutes return
  For the valley: 45 minutes

A short walk from the road through a stark rocky landscape leads to the fossil of a baleen whale. The fossil is very clear and is protected by Perspex from both the weather and prying fingers. Very helpful to the amateur is an interpretive board explaining exactly which parts of the whale are visible. If you have the time, it is worthwhile strolling down to the valley lined by ancient limestone rock formations.

8 Maori Rock Art   Easy   🚶   10 minutes return

- ✳ Accessible and sheltered rock drawing site including a post-European contact specimen.
- ➤ Just east of Duntroon on SH83, turn into Livingstone–Duntroon Road and the drawings are 500 metres on the left.

Located just above the road, a long rock overhang shelters numerous Maori rock drawings. Some are of animals while others are highly stylised, and a depiction of a European ship indicates that the practice of rock drawing continued into colonial times. Just north of Duntroon at Takiroa on SH83 is another easily accessible rock art site with startling red and black drawings.

9 Kurow Hill Hard 𝄍 1¼ hours return

* Wonderful views over the Waitaki Valley, Hunters Hills and the Hakataramea Valley.

➤ From SH83 in Kurow, go north past the shops in the town and then turn left into Grey Street. The track begins at the end of this street.

After crossing the irrigation channel at the end of Grey Street the track zigzags up the face of Kurow Hill, and while this is a solid uphill climb, the path is well graded and the walk well within the reach of the moderately fit. As you climb, Kurow township gradually recedes to toy-town dimensions, while the grand view over the Waitaki Valley unfurls. The vegetation is spare in the dry and exposed location, so the prospects are continuous as you climb.

About two-thirds of the way up the hill the track forks at an unmarked junction. At this point continue to the left, and near the top as the track reaches a ridge you again need to continue to the left to reach the summit. While the top of the hill can be very exposed in windy weather, the views are magnificent: over the length of the braided Waitaki River and beyond to the rolling hills of the Hakataramea Valley, and north-east to the Hunters Hills.

10 Moeraki Boulders Easy

* Perfectly rounded boulders lie scattered along this wild ocean beach.

➤ Signposted from SH1 just north of the turn-off to Moeraki village.

𝄍 From the car park: 20 minutes return
From the village: 1 hour return

Best seen at low tide, the Moeraki boulders are an unusual geological formation known as septarian concretion, the result of erosion exposing the more resistant stone in the shape of almost perfect round boulders, which now lie scattered along the beach. In Maori legend the boulders are the gourds washed overboard from the voyaging waka *Araiteuru* that arrived here around 1000 years ago.

North and East Otago

While most people stop by the beach, hop out for a quick walk and then move on, an attractive alternative is to drive into the picturesque little fishing village of Moeraki itself and park at the beginning of the Millennium Track. From here it is an hour return to the boulders on the beach.

11 Katiki Point Easy 🚶 45 minutes return

* Awesome coastal views, an historic pa site, a nineteenth-century lighthouse, and a great hide for penguin watching.

➤ Turn off SH1 at Moeraki and then turn right into Tenby Street, which becomes Lighthouse Road. Drive 3 km to the end of this gravel road.

The walk begins at the elegant wooden Moeraki lighthouse constructed in 1878. It was originally intended for Hokitika, but numerous shipwrecks along this tempestuous coast convinced the authorities to construct it at Moeraki. The views are amazing: north to Cape Wanbrow near Oamaru and south to Shag Point, and glimpses to the Otago Peninsula even further beyond.

The track then leads downhill to the superb pa site located on a narrow spur of land and almost encompassed by sea. Although very little now remains to be seen, this historic pa, known as Te Raka a Hineatea, was established in the eighteenth century and resisted many attempts at capture.

Just below the lighthouse is a large fenced area of coastal vegetation where a short track leads down to a small sandy cove overlooked by an excellent hide complete with binoculars! Both blue and yellow-eyed penguins nest here and the beach is also home to fur seals.

12 Trotters Gorge

* Lush bush reserve featuring a secluded cave and an appealing swimming hole.

➤ 2 km south of Moeraki on SH1, turn off into Horse Range Road. The picnic area from where the walks begin is on the right, but is not well signposted so it is easy to drive past.

A 152-hectare reserve on the southern end of Horse Range, Trotters Gorge is a popular picnic spot and walking area, although the complete absence of any signage, track information or track markings is not helpful. The deep gorge lush with bush is very attractive, and while the rocks in this area may look like limestone, they are in fact a greywacke/breccia conglomerate.

Cave Walk   Easy   🚶   30 minutes return

From the grass car park take the track to the left just past the toilets hidden in the trees. Follow the stream through dense bush, passing a rocky overhang. An unmarked track goes to the right but continue straight ahead. A short distance on, a shallow cave is reached deep in a narrow valley thick with beautiful native bush and surrounded by high rocky bluffs.

Trotters Creek   Easy   🚶   45 minutes return

A broad path continues across the stream from the car park and is a flat walk all the way through bush to a lovely grassy picnic area overlooking a large attractive swimming hole in Trotters Creek. A rustic shelter provides a refuge if the weather isn't so good. There are six stream crossings along this track, so it will be a challenge to keep your feet dry. The birdlife is prolific and the fluting of bellbirds is almost constant.

13   Puketapu Summit/John McKenzie Memorial
Hard   🚶   1 hour return

✳ Splendid views from this prominent hill topped by a memorial to a reforming local politician.

➤ The track begins in Stour Street, signposted from SH1 at the northern end of Palmerston township.

A steep climb leads to an unusual monument erected on the summit of Puketapu (343 metres) to the memory of local politician Sir John McKenzie. McKenzie was a champion of the small farmer and as a politician was instrumental in breaking up the huge landholdings that existed in the late nineteenth century. Built in 1931 (an earlier monument collapsed) of local bluestone, the cairn is 13 metres high and has an internal staircase. The view from the top is spectacular. For the very fit a race to the top is held in October in memory of local policeman Albert Kelly, who during the Second World War hiked to the top of the hill every day to scout the local coastline for signs of the enemy.

North and East Otago

14 Waikouaiti Beach and Hawkesbury Reserve Lagoon

Easy   🚶   1 hour

* ✷ Diverse birdlife abounds close to the bright white sands of Waikouaiti Beach.

* ➤ Turn off SH1 at Waikouaiti onto Beach Road and go to the very end and park at the beach. Walk back down the road to the railway line and turn right into Scotia Street. The walk begins at the end of this road.

The walk starts across the causeway through the lagoon, and at the end of the lagoon turn right (don't cross the footbridge). Continue along the second causeway and at the end take the track along the river and through the pine trees to the beach. Follow the beach back to the car park or spend however long you want on the beach.

What makes this walk particularly appealing is that the causeways cut right through the middle of the lagoon, with the birds just metres away. A wide range of wetland and wading birds make their home here including stilt, paradise duck, Canada goose, black swan, mallard and heron. The beach is a broad sweep of white sand protected by high headlands at either end.

15 Huriawa Pa, Karitane Beach   Easy   🚶   45 minutes

* ✷ An historic and spectacularly sited pa commands magnificent views along the coast.

* ➤ From SH1, turn off towards Karitane and take the road right to the beach. At the beach, turn left along Sulisker Street and continue 500 metres uphill to the pa entrance.

Volcanic in origin, with steep cliffs and sea on three sides, Huriawa Peninsula was the perfect location for a fortified pa, giving its defenders unimpeded views along the coast both north and south and over the estuarine marshes to the east. A Ngai Tahu stronghold, in the eighteenth century the pa resisted a protracted siege of over six months.

The entrance to the pa is through a beautifully carved gateway, and the track meanders gently to the end of the peninsula with superb views along the coast in both directions. Hooker's sea lions and fur seals are common along the shore, and there are several blowholes on the south side of the pa.

16 Mapoutahi Pa and Doctor's Point

Easy 🚶 1¼ hours return

* A journey through sea caves leads to an old pa site with sweeping coastal views (tide dependent).

➤ Turn off SH1 at Waitati and turn left to get to Doctor's Point Road. Follow this road to the end and park by the beach.

From the car park, walk down the beach and head south (right) and around Doctor's Point, passing through sea caves on the way. From here the views along the coast are marvellous towards Karitane to the north. This walk can only be undertaken at mid to low tide, and even at those times there is a short scramble over a rock slide that has tumbled down from the coastal cliffs.

The site of the pa is nothing short of perfect. Steep cliffs and a very narrow access point made the fortification easy to defend, while the sea and wide lagoons both north and south provided an excellent food resource. In either direction the views are extensive: Orokonui Lagoon and the Otago Peninsula to the south, and Purakaunui Inlet immediately to the north with Huriawa Pa glimpsed in the distance. Blue penguins nest above the white sandy beaches and aquatic birdlife is prolific.

17 Orokonui Ecosanctuary and Reserve
New Zealand's Tallest Tree Easy 🚶 1 hour return

* A towering Australian gum tree steals top spot as New Zealand's tallest tree.

➤ Turn off SH1 at Waitati and head for Port Chalmers for 1 km, then turn left into Orokonui Road and travel for 11 km. The car park is on the left just 50 metres before Orokonui Park (note: this park is private property).

No towering totara or kahikatea holds pride of place as New Zealand's tallest tree, but an Aussie import, *Eucalyptus regans*. Reaching almost 70 metres tall, the tree is in a large grove of gums that were self-sown from the ash of a fire in 1900. The track intially skirts the Orokonui lagoon and farmland and then follows a stream, the banks of which are planted in native trees by schools, and come complete with plant identification signs.

Surrounded by a predator-resistant fence, the ecosanctuary includes mature podocarps as well as kaikawaka, or New Zealand cedar. Recently South Island kaka, saddleback, robin and jeweled gecko have been reintroduced.

Dunedin and Otago Peninsula

Waitati

Port Chalmers

Otago Harbour

Portobello

Dunedin

Otago Peninsula

Dunedin City and Port Chalmers

1 Mt Cargill and the Organ Pipes Medium

✱ Magnificent views from the top of Mt Cargill taking in the volcanic rocks of the Organ Pipes en route.

➤ From North East Valley follow North Road. From the point where North Road eventually morphs into Mt Cargill Road, the car park is 3 km on the left, but there is very limited parking space.

🚶 Organ Pipes: 40 minutes return

Mt Cargill: 2 hours return

All the hard climbing on this walk comes in the first 15 minutes as the track goes solidly uphill with quite a few steps before levelling off. From there it is a surprisingly easy walk to Mt Cargill, well within the capabilities of anyone with reasonable fitness, and with just another short uphill stretch at the very top. The early part of the walk is through fine bush, ferns and mosses.

Not far from the start, what at first look like carefully shaped steps are in fact natural and are broken rock from the formation known as the Organ Pipes. The pipes are basalt rock of volcanic origin that has been shaped in the cooling process into very precise geometric forms. The formation is not easy to see properly, but the jumble of broken rock below the pipes is interesting in itself.

From the Organ Pipes, the track leads through more subalpine vegetation to the top of Mt Cargill, where a cairn indicates all the key geographical features. The 360-degree views over Dunedin and the coast north and south from this 676-metre peak are spectacular. Mt Cargill is very exposed and often shrouded in cloud, so if the weather isn't too flash don't bother with the hike as you won't see a thing; however, if the day dawns fine be sure to make this your first priority.

2 Historic Dunedin Easy 🚶 Allow 1 hour

✱ Some of the finest Victorian and early twentieth-century buildings in New Zealand.

➤ Begin this walk in the Octagon, Dunedin City centre.

With the advent of the gold rushes inland, Dunedin quickly became the boom town of New Zealand in the second half of the nineteenth century. Along with all this quick money came merchants and bankers who also made their fortunes, and this prosperity was reflected in the grand buildings in Dunedin's commercial district. With the waning of the gold era, Dunedin's growth in the twentieth century slowed considerably, leaving the modern cityscape peppered with some of New Zealand's finest historic buildings.

This walk begins in the Octagon, heads south along Princes Street as far as Liverpool Street, then back along Princes Street to the Exchange. A short detour up Rattray Street leads to St Joseph's Cathedral. Once back at the Exchange, walk down High Street to the railway station and then back up Stuart Street to the Octagon.

Key sites and buildings along the way include:

- The Octagon. Dunedin has very cleverly ensured that the city's central public space, the Octagon, has remained people-friendly, with a mix of historic buildings, cafés, picture theatres and the smart city art gallery. The magnificent Municipal Buildings were designed by Robert Lawson and completed in 1880. Considerably altered in 1939 and 1963, the historic structure is now completely restored with its 40-metre-high clock tower dominating its surrounds. In the heart of the Octagon is a statue of the Scottish poet Robert Burns, unveiled in 1886 to a crowd of over 8000 people and today the venue for poetry reading on the bard's birthday, the 25th of January.

- Princes Street. At one time the heart of Dunedin's commercial district, Princes Street has now been somewhat left behind as the central retail area has moved north along George Street. Major buildings in Princes Street include the ANZ Bank (1874), Bank of New Zealand (1883), National Bank (1912), old Post Office (1937), Union Bank (1874) and Wains Hotel (1878).

- First Church of Otago. Just off Princes Street in Moray Place is one of New Zealand's most elegant buildings, the First Church of Otago. Opened in 1873 and built of Oamaru stone on a base of local volcanic rock, the church was designed by prominent local architect Robert Lawson. The visitors' centre at the back of the church has a display of the beautiful original architectural drawings as well as historical photographs of the house of worship under construction.

- The Exchange. The Exchange was the hub of the financial area and has at its centre the very elaborate Cargill Memorial honouring founding settler William Cargill. Moved to the Exchange in 1872 and converted to a very grand drinking fountain, the monument was originally erected in the Octagon in 1863.

- St Joseph's Cathedral. Just uphill from the Exchange on the corner of Rattray and Smith Streets, and built in bluestone, St Joseph's Cathedral (opened 1886) was designed in the Gothic Revival style by renowned church architect F. W. Petre, in direct contrast to his Romanesque-style churches in Christchurch, Invercargill, Waimate and Oamaru.

- Dunedin Railway Station. From the Exchange, walk down High Street to the railway station, taking time to view Dunedin Prison, built of brick in 1896 (and still a prison), before crossing the road to admire the distinct art deco lines of the New Zealand Rail Road Service building completed in 1937 and now part of the Otago Settlers Museum.

  Built in 1906, Dunedin Railway Station was at that time the largest and busiest terminal in the country. The two-storey building is in the Flemish Renaissance style and constructed of dark volcanic stone and the lighter Oamaru limestone, with stunning Royal Doulton tiles in the foyer. The mosaic flooring, magnificent stained-glass windows and Edwardian ironwork along the platform are all original.

- Law Courts. Lower Stuart Street, linking Dunedin Railway Station to the Octagon, houses the Law Courts, built in the Flemish Renaissance style (like the railway station) in 1899.

3 Ross Creek Reservoir Easy 🧍 45 minutes return

✳ A bush-fringed Victorian reservoir still supplies Dunedin City with water.

➤ The walk begins just over the bridge on Rockside Road near the intersection with Malvern Street, north Dunedin.

The Ross Creek Reservoir was built in 1867 to supply the rapidly growing Otago settlement. Still in use today, the reservoir's distinct Victorian valve tower and earth dam are the oldest in existence and fine old stone walls still line the dam. The reservoir is recognised as an outstanding engineering achievement by IPENZ (Institute of Professional Engineers New Zealand).

The gentle uphill walk to the reservoir is part of the much longer Leith

Valley walkway and wends its way through a mix of introduced and native trees, including some very large native tree fuchsias. On reaching the dam the walk then becomes a flat loop around the reservoir.

4 Woodhaugh Gardens Easy ⃛ 30 minutes

* ✳ An attractive mix of native trees and formal gardens in the city centre.
* ➤ North end of George Street just before Pine Hill Road, Dunedin.

A rambling combination of bush, grassy picnic spots, ponds and playgrounds, this is in fact a rare native forest remnant within walking distance of the motel strip on George Street. The flat paths and tracks meander through 12 hectares alongside the lovely Water of Leith (also known as the Leith River or Leith Stream) and is an ideal spot for the kids to let off a little steam.

5 Dunedin Botanic Gardens Easy

* ✳ The oldest botanic gardens in New Zealand are made for walking.
* ➤ Cumberland Street, north Dunedin.
* ⃛ Lower garden: Allow 45 minutes
  Lower and upper gardens: Allow 1¼ hours

Established in 1863, these are the oldest botanic gardens in New Zealand and fall naturally into two parts. The older section is flat and laid out more formally with rose gardens, Edwardian winter house, children's playground with a Peter Pan statue, and a duck pond. The herbaceous borders thrive in the cooler climate and are the best in the land. At their peak between December and February, the perennial long borders arranged in blue, red, violet, white and yellow are stunning. In summer there is live music in the band rotunda on Sunday afternoons and in the heart of the gardens is a café and information centre.

Across the Water of Leith, which divides the gardens, is the larger upper section, much less formal and planted with bigger trees and shrubs, including 4 hectares of rhododendrons and azaleas. This section also contains the very attractive modern bird aviaries, which are worth the hike in themselves. Among the birds is a collection of New Zealand parrots including kea, kaka and yellow-fronted, red-crowned and the rare Antipodes Island kakariki.

6 Port Chalmers   Easy   🚶   1 hour

✳ Take in the sights on a perambulation about Otago's historic port.

➤ Start at the Port Chalmers Museum, Beach Street, Port Chalmers.

The upper harbour at Dunedin is too shallow and the channel too narrow for anything other than small boats. So, from the beginning of European settlement in 1844, Port Chalmers was developed as the port for the city, making it New Zealand's third-oldest town. Like Dunedin, it has many fine stone buildings, most erected between 1874 and 1880; and while these include churches and banks, Port Chalmers also has several great old pubs including Carey's Bay Hotel (1874), Chicks Hotel (1876), and Port Chalmers Hotel (established 1846).

This walk begins at the Museum (originally the Post Office, built 1877), and tends gently uphill via Grey Street and Scotia Street to the lookout, easily recognised by the mast of the old pirate ship the *Cincinnati*. After taking in the views over the wharves and town, go downhill to the right to the water's edge at Back Beach. From Back Beach, turn to the right and follow the shoreline as it meanders around the point with views the length of Otago Harbour. The track then leads back to the main street, passing the historic buildings in the town centre along the way.

7 Aramoana Breakwater   Easy   🚶   1 hour

✳ A white sandy beach and a long breakwater stand at the entrance to Otago Harbour.

➤ From Port Chalmers continue east along the Otago Harbour to the very end of the road.

Safeguarding the entrance to Otago Harbour, this long breakwater was primarily constructed to stop the channel silting up. Ideally you should time your visit to watch a ship enter or leave the harbour, but even without this attraction, the breakwater is a fine place for a stroll, especially with a heavy swell rolling in from the east. Take binoculars and you might even spot an albatross in flight from the colony just opposite on Taiaroa Head, and fur seals and blue penguins are not uncommon here either.

Just inside the breakwater a track and boardwalk lead through the tidal salt marshes, home to numerous wading birds including godwits in the summer months, while to the north of the breakwater the wide sandy beach of Aramoana is ideal for a leisurely beach amble.

8 Tunnel Beach   Medium   🚶 1 hour return

* A short tunnel drops down to a cove on this dramatic stretch of coastline.

➤ Near the end of Blackhead Road, St Clair, south Dunedin.

The walk begins with a downhill slope over farmland towards a natural sea arch. From the top of the arch there are marvellous views south along the coast, and in wild weather waves pound the rocks below – the greater the swell, the more impressive the wave action! A low tunnel with shallow steps leads down from the top of the arch to a small cove of pristine white sand, particularly attractive at low tide. John Cargill, son of the prominent settler William Cargill, built this tunnel so that his daughters could go swimming away from the more public beach at St Clair. Unfortunately, one of the daughters drowned here, so needless to say the sea is not safe for swimming.

Otago Peninsula

The rugged nature of the Otago Peninsula, an ancient volcano, has a character all of its own, with magnificent beaches and spectacular cliffs, and supports a unique wildlife that includes albatross, seals, and both blue and yellow-eyed penguins. In pre-European times the peninsula was home to a large Maori population, mainly clustered along the warmer, north-facing southern shores. The calm waters of the harbour drew Europeans too, and Scots in particular made the region their own. Today the peninsula is laced with narrow roads, hugging the sea along the shore of the harbour, and traversing high ridges with spectacular views over the wild Southern Ocean.

In recent years, penguin watching on the peninsula has become popular, especially for the rare yellow-eyed penguin or hoiho, of which fewer than 4000 now remain. These solitary and unsociable birds construct nests in coastal vegetation up to 1 km inland that affords the shelter and privacy they require. Eggs are laid in September and hatch about six weeks later, though the chicks are not fully independent until around March.

Unfortunately, the number of visitors has unintentionally put stress on the very wildlife they have come to see. The penguins are easily disturbed by people or animals coming between them and their nests, and if distressed will quickly return to the sea leaving the chicks unfed. There are hides at both Sandfly Bay and Pilots Bay, and if you see penguins on the beach, move quietly and allow them direct access from the water back to the nests behind the beach.

9 Glenfalloch Woodland Garden Easy ⅄ Allow 1 hour

✳ A magnificent garden in the classic English woodland style.

➤ 430 Portobello Road, Otago Peninsula.

Established in 1871 by George Russell, and originally only accessible by sea, the homestead at Glenfalloch was constructed of kauri and Baltic pine. Some of the trees were planted as early as 1872, and over the years the garden has grown substantially in both size and diversity. Philip Barling, the owner from 1917 to 1956, set about replicating the perfect English woodland garden and primarily created the environs seen today. Philip's son John, who inherited the garden on his father's death, then added his own touch by planting the rhododendrons and azaleas.

Now covering over 12 hectares, the garden is a maze of interconnecting paths to suit every level of fitness, though be warned that some parts are quite steep. There is a café open during summer and a small entrance fee applies.

10 Karetai Trig Medium ⅄ 45 minutes return

✳ Magnificent views south along the coast from this cliff-top trig.

➤ The track begins at the end of Karetai Road, Smails Beach, Otago Peninsula.

A steady uphill trudge through farmland leads to a cliff-top trig with excellent views west over the city beaches: Smails, Tomahawk, St Kilda and St Clair. Far to the south in the distance lies Nugget Point, and to the east along the coast sheer cliff faces plunge into a rugged sea. This is a good spot to watch seabirds as they wheel far below along the wave-lashed cliffs.

11 Sandymount

✳ Several tracks lead from the car park high on this dune that has some of the best coastal scenery on the peninsula.

➤ End of Sandymount Road off Highcliff Road, which is the main road running along the top ridge of the peninsula.

Lover's Leap and The Chasm   Easy   🚶   50 minutes return

The walk begins through a short avenue of old macrocarpa and then crosses tussock farmland with marvellous views over Allans Beach, Hoopers and Papanui Inlets and Mt Charles along the way.

The Chasm is a massive vertical drop to a rock base and beyond that the foaming sea. Oddly enough, there is a car wreck at the very bottom (not visible from the top), though how it got there is anyone's guess as there is no road access to this point. From the Chasm it is a short walk to Lover's Leap, a sheer cliff face that drops to a large sea arch. From both lookout points the views along the high cliffs on the southern coast of the peninsula are fantastic. In windy weather it can be very exposed, so come prepared.

Sandymount Summit   Medium   🚶   25 minutes return

A rough track leads up from the car park to the 319-metre summit with panoramic views. From here you can see south to Nugget Point, north to Moeraki, and catch just a glimpse of Dunedin City. A basic track leads from the summit around to Lover's Leap for those wanting a longer walk.

12 Sandfly Bay   Easy   🚶   1 hour return

✳ Wind-blown sand is responsible for the apt name of this exposed bay.

➤ The walk starts from the end of Ridge Road, to the left off Sandymount Road.

While you can walk to Sandfly Bay from Sandymount, the quicker option for those short on time is to drive back along Sandymount Road, take Ridge Road to the left and drive to the very end (make sure you don't block the entrance to the farm when you park and note that the track is closed for lambing from 1 September to 1 November).

The track initially crosses farmland and then enters dune country that has spread a surprising way inland along this valley, driven by the fierce southerly winds. Consequently, the beach takes its name not from the pesky insect but the incidence of this wind-blown sand. The beautiful wide beach of white sand is flanked by steep cliffs at either end, and offshore lie several small rock stacks. Yellow-eyed penguin (hoiho) nest in the extensive dunes and seals are also common on the beach.

13 Allans Beach Easy 🚶 10 minutes return

* Hoiho nest in the lupins behind this charming sandy beach.

➤ From Portobello, turn right into Harington Point Road and after 2 km turn right into Weir Road. Then, after 1.5 km, turn into Papanui Inlet Road, and after a further 2 km right into Cape Saunders Road. About 1 km down this road turn right into Allans Beach Road and continue to the very end. The track begins just past the woolshed.

This is a short easy walk to a beach where in the late afternoon penguins can be seen making their way back to their nests in the dunes behind the beach.

If you are feeling very fit you can clamber to the top of Mt Charles, at 408 metres the highest point on the peninsula. This track begins about 500 metres back down the road from the beach, but it crosses private property and you need to phone for permission first (ph 03 478 0274).

14 Okia Reserve/Victory Beach Easy 🚶 1½ hours return

* Two small pyramid-shaped hills guard the approaches to a magnificent sweep of white-sand beach.

➤ Just beyond Portobello village turn right into Weir Road and follow this road to the end. It is a gravel road but in reasonable condition.

Beginning through farmland, this walk then passes through the Pyramids, two aptly named small hills that are volcanic in origin. Take a careful look at the seaward side of the small pyramid, and the volcanic basalt columns precise in their geometric patterning are very obvious (similar to the Organ Pipes on Mt Cargill). There is also a short scramble to the top of the smaller pyramid for a view over the dune country.

From the Pyramids, the track continues through wetland and dune terrain to the beach. Take care in the scrub-covered dunes behind the beach as Hooker's sea lions, easily camouflaged, use them to rest. They are not called sea lions for nothing and can be quite aggressive when disturbed. Penguins also nest in the dunes; give them plenty of latitude.

The beach takes its name from the ship *Victory* that came to grief on the shore while under the command of a proverbial drunken sailor, though very little now remains of the wreck. The beach is totally undeveloped, open to the Southern Ocean, and is about as pristine as it possibly gets on the peninsula.

Central Otago

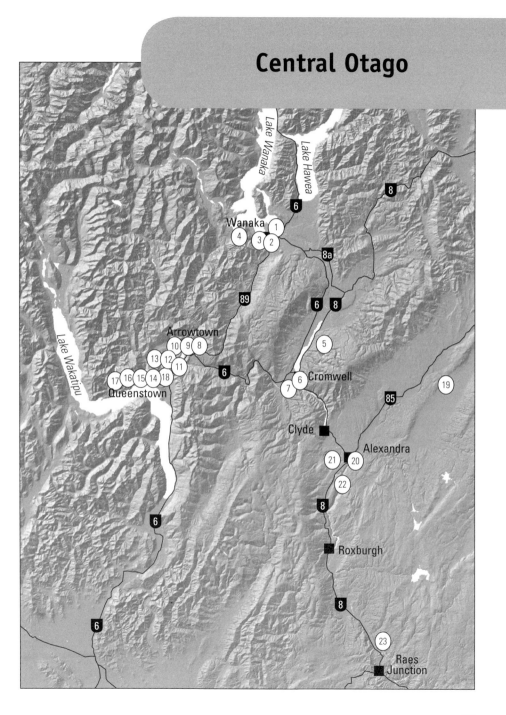

Wanaka

1 Clutha River Outlet   Easy   🚶   1¼ hours return

   ✻ Walkers and anglers can both appreciate the pure and swift-running Clutha as it leaves Lake Wanaka.

   ➤ 5 km east of Wanaka, turn left towards Albert Town (West Coast Road). After 500 metres turn left into Aubrey Road and at the roundabout turn right into Gunn Road. The track begins at the corner of Gunn Road and Alison Avenue.

The Clutha has the largest water flow of any New Zealand river, and here at the outlet of Lake Wanaka the water runs swift and clean. The track follows a gentle path all the way from Albert Town to the outlet and is partially shaded by willows. This section of the river is much favoured by fisher folk and is famous for large brown and rainbow trout and Chinook salmon.

2 Mt Iron   Medium   🚶   1½ hours

   ✻ Fantastic views from this glacial mountain overlooking Wanaka.

   ➤ 1 km east of Wanaka on the main road to the airport.

A popular walk with visitors and locals alike, at 548 metres Mt Iron stands isolated from the surrounding mountains and therefore offers excellent views in every direction. The mountain bears the scars of earlier times when this landscape was scoured by massive glaciers. Known as a 'roche moutonnée', glaciers have ridden over the western side of the mountain leaving it relatively smooth, while the east side has been sharply scraped away.

To take advantage of the easier grade it is best to walk this loop track clockwise, up the gentler western slope and down the steep eastern side. The open nature of the low vegetation ensures endless views all the way, while at the top the prospects extend in all directions: south along Cardrona Valley, east to the broad terraces of the Clutha River, north over Lake Hawea, west across Lake Wanaka and beyond to the Southern Alps.

Top The Fox Glacier tears a rock-strewn path down a steep-sided valley.
Above Set in a magnificent wilderness, Okarito is home to the mystical white heron and the elusive Okarito brown kiwi.

Top The Mirror Lakes or 'tarns' reflecting the surrounding mountains offer a popular short stop on the road to Fiordland Sound.

Above Munro Beach in Westland is not only wild and bracing but also home to the rare Fiordland crested penguin.

Top A walk along the shores of Lake Wanaka is rewarded with dramatic mountain prospects.
Above Rippon Vineyard is a short detour from the shores of Lake Wanaka on the Waterfall
Creek walk.

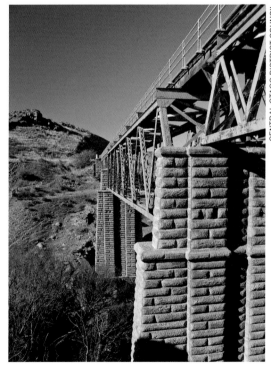

Top The dry climate of Central Otago creates crystalline open landscapes unique in New Zealand.

Above The Chinese Settlement walk at Arrowtown gives a glimpse of life on the old goldfields.

Right Superbly constructed from local stone, the Poolburn Viaduct is just one of the highlights on a walk along the Otago Central Rail Trail.

TOURISM DUNEDIN

Above The centrally located Octagon is the ideal spot for a café stop before taking a walk in historic Dunedin. Today, some of this country's most impressive Victorian and Edwardian architecture lies within a short walk of the central precinct.

Right Built in 1906 and recognised as an historic building of international importance, the Dunedin Railway Station is wonderfully preserved.

TOURISM DUNEDIN

Above Otago Harbour: Careys Bay (top) is home to a small fishing fleet in historic Port Chalmers. Rare yellowed-eyed penguins (left) nest on Otago Peninsula's many beautiful beaches accessed by several short walks. Intriguing architectural details (right) reflect Port Chalmers' origins as Dunedin's main port.

GRAHAM DAINTY 'TE ANAU LAKEFRONT – AUTUMN' / DESTINATION FIORDLAND

Above From this walk along the shores of Lake Te Anau, the views across the water to the mountains of Fiordland are continuous.

Right Rich green mosses and lichens swathe the trees and forest floor on the gentle loop walk to Lake Gunn.

Top From the lookout at Tussock Creek in Central Southland, the views extend south to Stewart Island and north and west to the mountain peaks.
Above A golden sunset over the New River Estuary from the walks on Sandy Point, Invercargill.

3 Waterfall Creek   Easy

✳ Views of the mountains and lake from the shoreline and a trip to a vineyard.

➤ From Wanaka town centre, follow the lake shore to the Wanaka Station Park at the western end of Roys Bay. The track begins right by the water.

🚶 From the western end of the lake-front park: 1 hour return

From the town centre: 2 hours return

Beginning at Wanaka Station Park (an excellent place for a picnic), this easy flat walk follows the lake shore with pleasant views over Lake Wanaka to the mountains. At Waterfall Creek (a creek but no waterfall) the walk ends at a wide shingle beach. A popular detour is up through the Rippon Vineyard for a spot of wine tasting. The views over the vineyard to the lake and mountains are stunning, and even more so when the vines turn golden in autumn.

A word of warning – some mountain bikers barrel along this track, so be prepared for a quick dive into the bushes to avoid being knocked down.

4 Diamond Lake

✳ Aerial views of Lake Wanaka and the Matukituki River.

➤ 20 km from Wanaka on the Mt Aspiring Road and 6 km past the Glendhu Bay camping ground. The turn-off to the track is just before the bridge over the Motatapu River.

🚶 Diamond Lake: Easy, 25 minutes return

Lake Wanaka lookout: Medium, 1 hour return

Lake circuit: Medium, 2 hours return

Central Otago

The track starts off gently uphill towards the small Diamond Lake that reflects the surrounding landscape in its raupo-fringed waters. From this point the track climbs more steeply through bush to a dramatic bluff overlooking the pocket-sized lake far below. A little further beyond, the track goes off to the right to the Wanaka lookout with views over Lake Wanaka and the Matukituki River. From here, the going gets rougher as the track meanders up the scrubby hillside to the top of Rocky Mountain (775 metres) to even more spectacular views of the Wanaka Basin. The track, on the southern side of Rocky Mountain, is totally shaded in winter and therefore can be icy.

Cromwell

5 Bendigo Goldfields

✸ Well-preserved mining relics set against a picturesque high-altitude backdrop.

➤ From Cromwell, take SH8 towards Tarras, and after 14 km turn right into Bendigo Loop Road. Continue down this road a further 2 km then turn right at Bendigo township to Welshtown. The road beyond Bendigo deteriorates rapidly, especially between Logantown and Welshtown, and you might prefer to park at Logantown (recognisable by the wooden wagon) and walk the short distance uphill to Welshtown.

Matilda Battery   Easy   🚶   40 minutes

Thomas Logan discovered gold in these parts in 1863, and the whole area is a labyrinth of mine shafts, old townships and ruined batteries hidden among the rocks and tussock. This loop walk, starting at Welshtown, has some of the best-preserved miners' huts in Central Otago, several of which are only missing their roof.

The walk wends its way through tussock and scrub past mine shafts, old rock walks and ruined miners' cottages to the Matilda Battery. Opened in 1878, the shaft at Matilda went down 178 metres, and the 16-stamper battery, powered by steam, crushed the ore hauled up from the depths. The mine closed in 1884, and in 1908 ten of the stampers were relocated to the nearby Come In Time battery where they remain to this day.

A bonus on the walk is the magnificent vistas over the Tarras area and the mountains to the west and north. Many of the deep shafts in the locale are not covered, so keep a close eye on youngsters if you don't want to lose them down some deep dark hole!

Pengelly's Hotel Walk   Easy   🚶   20 minutes return

The ruins of this tiny hotel are visible from the car park, but are worth a closer look as they are some of the most substantial in the area. From the car park, follow the 4WD road and cross the dam to the hotel. After visiting the hotel continue up the creek and past the ruins of several miners' huts and back to the car park. Pengelly's Hotel is incredibly small, with rooms so tiny that it is hard to imagine them holding any more than three or four burly miners, let alone a bar!

Central Otago

6 Cromwell Old Reservoir and Firewood Creek

Medium 🚶 50 minutes return

✳ A wild rocky landscape and excellent views over Cromwell and Lake Dunstan.

➤ Opposite the Cromwell Lookout on SH8, 1.5 km south of the bridge over Lake Dunstan at Cromwell.

Lake Dunstan was created by the construction of the Clyde Dam during the 1980s and officially opened in 1994. The dam flooded not only the old town of Cromwell and its famous gorge, but also large areas of fertile river flats, bringing Lake Dunstan into existence in the process. Key historic buildings were removed and reconstructed above the water level, but the old stone bridge over the gorge remains intact, albeit 11 metres below the surface of the lake. According to local legend a car is still parked on it.

Starting 50 metres from the Cromwell Lookout on the other side of the road, the track is moderately steep, ascending steadily through a sparse landscape of rock and wild thyme to an old reservoir. Now dry, this stone-lined reservoir once supplied the town with water, and the exit pipes and depth-measuring posts are still in place, as well as the supply pipe, which is visible at several points along the track. The views are superb, encompassing Lake Dunstan, Cromwell town surrounded by vineyards, and beyond that the Pisa Range.

Above the reservoir, the landscape is a sea of rocky outcrops, tors and loose stones, and even the wild thyme struggles to survive on these bone-dry slopes, which are a far cry from the country's more familiar lush bush landscapes. In fact, the herb thyme in Central Otago is thought to be the only wild population outside its natural range in the Mediterranean. Most likely introduced by miners during the gold-rush era, thyme has thrived in the harsh dry climate of Central Otago and its distinct bouquet is now a signature of the local landscape.

Having put the steepest part of the walk behind you, you head gently uphill to a 4WD track, and then downhill for a short section before joining another track to the right and back to the road.

Central Otago

✳ Carved entirely by human toil, this barren landscape will not fail to fascinate.

➤ Well signposted in Felton Road, Bannockburn.

人 To Stewart Town: 1 hour return
   For the loop walk: 1½ hours

The Sluicings is an amazing area of cliffs, gulches, pinnacles, tunnels and old ruins set amid a barren landscape and all man-made. In the late nineteenth century, technology enabled gravelly soils to be worked with high-pressure sluicing hoses resulting in a drastic revision of the topography. Blasted by water, the flat terrain near Bannockburn has been altered beyond recognition and has a strange appeal all of its own. This is a great place to either work up an appetite or walk off a lunch at one of the excellent vineyards close by.

The walk begins gently uphill through a deep gully stacked high with rock debris from the sluicing, and with tunnels leading deep into the base of the fluted cliffs. From here, the climb leads to a flat terrace with grapevines that was the original level of the land prior to the mining era, which began in the 1880s. A short walk takes you to Stewart Town, containing a small handful of ruins. Almost intact, and with only the roof missing, is the small cottage that was home to David Stewart and John Menzies, both bachelors, who made their money by providing the vital water supply on which the miners depended. Surrounding the house are old apple and pear trees that still bear fruit. Just to the east of the dwelling, a number of distinct channels, which carried the water from the dam to the workings, are still clearly visible. From Stewart Town, the loop walk follows a parallel valley to the east, past the remains of a blacksmith's forge and miners' huts.

Especially welcome on this walk are the information boards that for once are written for adults and not the typical signage worded as though for the less intellectually gifted child!

Arrowtown

Gold was discovered in the Arrow River bed in 1862 by shearer Jack Tewa, and a shantytown was quickly established close to the river only to be washed away in a flood the following year. The settlement was rebuilt on higher ground, and the population swiftly rose to over 7000, with further settlements at Macetown, Skippers and Bullendale. Today, over 60 buildings remain from the gold-mining period including a row of quaint miners' cottages dwarfed by huge old trees well over a hundred years old.

The cool Central Otago climate makes it one of the few places in New Zealand to experience spectacular autumn colour, and this is one of the best times to visit the area, being between the summer peak and the winter ski season. Around Arrowtown are several walks of varying lengths, and they all start by the river behind the shops in the main street, Buckingham Street.

8 Chinese Settlement Walk   Easy 𝕏 30 minutes return

✻ The life of the Chinese miner on a New Zealand goldfield recreated.

➤ Signposted from the car park by the river behind the Buckingham Street shops.

The Chinese goldminers occupied the margins of society both socially and physically, and although 1200 Chinese arrived to rework old claims in the Wakatipu Basin in 1869, very little remains of their humble abodes. However, at Arrowtown the small Chinese section of town has been preserved and in some places reconstructed. As well as simple stone cottages there is a tiny store, and the excellent information panels enhance this easy walk.

9 Otago 150th Anniversary Walkway
Easy 𝕏 1¼ hours return

✻ An attractive tree-screened ramble along the banks of the Arrow River.

➤ Signposted from the car park by the river behind the Buckingham Street shops.

This very pleasant flat walk on a good track starts along the near side of the clear and fast-flowing Arrow River, shaded by willow, sycamore and larch. After 10 minutes the track reaches a footbridge, and from this point the walk becomes a loop along both sides of the river. You can either cross this bridge or walk further on to the second bridge. On the western side of the river the track passes the site of the Criterion Quartz Reef mine established in the 1860s, though now nothing remains.

This is a very attractive shaded walk on a hot summer's day, and there are several small sandy beaches and swimming holes, some with rope swings.

Central Otago

10 Tobins Track   Medium 🚶 1½ hours return

* ✴ Expansive prospects of the Arrowtown Basin and surrounding ranges.

* ➤ Signposted from the car park by the river behind the Buckingham Street shops.

From the car park, follow the river downstream for about 10 minutes and then cross over the footbridge. From the bridge, the path goes steadily uphill on a well-graded 4WD track to the lookout. Initially the walk is through larch and sycamore, but about halfway up the trees begin to thin and extensive views gradually unfold over the Arrowtown Basin and the mountains beyond. The views from the top are superb and include the Remarkables, Arrowtown, Lake Hayes and Lake Wakatipu.

The land up here is surprisingly flat and was the site of Crown Terrace settlement, a substantial township in the 1860s to 1870s, though nothing now remains. Thomas Tobin, after whom the track is named, built the road to Crown Terrace in 1874, and lived on the road just uphill from the river. The ford by the bridge was the location of the famous Ringwraiths scene in the first Lord of the Rings film *The Fellowship of the Ring*.

Queenstown

11 Lake Hayes   Easy 🚶 1 hour return

* ✴ Take a gentle stroll beside the placid waters of picturesque and much photographed Lake Hayes.

* ➤ Begin at either the Recreation Ground on SH6 from Queenstown to Cromwell, just before the turn-off to Arrowtown, or at the large picnic area at the northern end of the lake.

Although this track is not marked at either end, it isn't hard to find as it follows the shoreline. At the northern end, the track begins where the access road to the picnic ground meets the main road, while at the Recreation Ground it starts to the right of the car park by the boat ramp.

Following the shoreline, the walk meanders along the lake under the shade of old willows and poplars and looks out upon tranquil views over the lake and the mountains. About halfway along is the pretty Bendemeer Reserve offering a grassy spot for a lakeside picnic. The reserve at the northern end of

Central Otago

the lake is particularly popular in summer as Lake Hayes is much shallower than the deep mountain lakes and the water not so cold for swimming. This is a great spot on a hot summer's day and is especially appealing in autumn with the trees dappled vivid yellow and gold.

12 Historic Shotover Bridge   Easy   🏃 45 minutes return

✳ An historic bridge over the Shotover River.

➤ On the Queenstown side of the new Shotover Bridge on SH6, turn into Tucker Beach Road and the old bridge is half a kilometre down this road.

The old Shotover Bridge was built in 1915 to replace an even older bridge that was swept away in the floods of 1878. From the bridge there are views in both directions along the river to Coronet Peak one way and the Remarkables in the other. Once across the bridge, drop down the track to the right, walk underneath the bridge and then upstream for as long as you like along the willow-shaded banks. This is a good spot for watching jet boats skim along the shallow waters of the Shotover, which was named by William Rees after the Shotover Estate in Oxfordshire, England.

13 Oxenbridge Tunnel   Easy   🏃 30 minutes return

✳ Commanding views over the Shotover River gorge.

➤ At the Shotover Bridge at Arthurs Point, turn into Oxenbridge Tunnel Road and continue along this narrow gravel road until it drops down to the river and a large sandy car park.

There are no signs indicating the track from the car park, but follow the river upstream for a short distance and the track becomes obvious.

This short walk along the Shotover River leads to a lookout point above the rugged gorge and the Oxenbridge Tunnel. The Oxenbridge brothers, whose intention was to divert the river and make a fortune from the gold in the riverbed, built the tunnel between 1906 and 1910. However, the scheme only returned a small amount of ore. Today this is a good perch from which to watch jets boats on the river below. Spot, too, the rusting steam engine strangely marooned on a rock in the middle of the river.

Central Otago

14 Time Walk, Queenstown Hill   Hard

✳ Bird's-eye views over Queenstown, Lake Wakatipu and the Remarkables from this hilltop height.

➤ Kerry Drive, Queenstown.

🚶 1 hour 40 minutes return
If walking up from the town: Add 30 minutes

A millennium project, the Time Walk is a solid uphill slog. Officially the walk begins at a beautiful wrought-iron gate and takes the walker from the past to the future, represented at the top by Caroline Robinson's simple sculpture *Basket of Dreams*. Along the way the story of the Wakatipu Basin is told in a series of five illustrated panels (that you will either find endearing or pretentious). To follow the panels you have to turn right at the junction where the track becomes a loop. This direction is also the gentler grade to the top.

At the small pond on top of the ridge veer left to the *Basket of Dreams* and the track downhill, or if you are feeling energetic having got this far, the track to the right will take you to the summit of Queenstown Hill (907 metres). Most of the walk is through pine and Douglas fir, with the occasional view glimpsed through the branches. However, near the top the vegetation is open and a grand view of the lake, mountains and town is laid out before you.

15 Queenstown Gardens   Easy 🚶 45 minutes return

✳ A little peninsula contains the long-established Queenstown Gardens.

➤ Accessible from central Queenstown by following the foreshore to the east of the town.

A combination of formal gardens, woodland walks and sports facilities, Queenstown Gardens occupies a small peninsula that juts out into the lake and from the tip of the gardens gives unspoiled views over the water to the mountains. Established in 1866 on land gifted to the public by Queenstown businessman Bendix Hallenstein, today the park contains some enormous mature trees. In easy walking distance of town, the gardens are just the place to walk off that lunch or dinner, or if you prefer, partake in a game of tennis or some ice skating.

16 Sunshine Bay   Easy   🚶   1½ hours return

✱ Views over the lake following a good walk from the town centre.

➤ From the centre of Queenstown, follow the shoreline of the lake west from the town.

Another pleasant walk from the centre of Queenstown, technically this walk commences at Fernhill just out of Queenstown on the Glenorchy Road, but is easily accessible from the town centre by following the footpath along the edge of the lake. The path eventually becomes a track along the road and then drops down below the road to wind along the lake, through a cool forest of mixed exotic and native trees. Beyond the trees, the track reaches Sunshine Bay, a small shingle beach with boat-launching facilities. On the way back don't walk along the road, as it is narrow, there is no footpath and the traffic is swift.

17 Bobs Cove   Easy   🚶   1¼ hours return

✱ Historic lime kilns on the lake edge lead to a lookout point over Wakatipu.

➤ 14 km from Queenstown on the Glenorchy Road.

From the car park, the track wanders downhill through a mixture of eucalypts and native trees to a small bay on the lake edged with white shingle and named after a local boatman, Bob Fortune. The track then follows the shoreline past several nineteenth-century lime kilns, one of which in particular is very well preserved. Limestone was an essential ingredient of the mortar used in local stonework in an area where stone rather than wood was the preferred building material. The gum trees may have been planted to provide a supply of wood to fuel the kilns.

Just past the kilns, the track divides. At this point take the right-hand fork as this is a more gradual climb to the top of the hill with only a short steep section near the summit. From up here the views are marvellous in all directions, with the bush-fringed shore below and the Remarkables rising high on the far side of the lake. After taking in the view, continue downhill and at the next junction take the fork to the left and return to the car park.

Central Otago

18 Kelvin Peninsula   Easy 🚶 1 hour return

✳ Wonderful views over the water and surrounding mountains from the end of a scenic peninsula.

➤ From SH6 heading south to Invercargill, turn right into Peninsula Road just after crossing the Kawarau River and follow the road to the very end where you reach the Kelvin Heights Golf Course. Follow the signs into the golf course and park immediately to the right by the lake beside the children's playground. While the track is not marked from the car park, it begins along the lake shore to the left and isn't hard to find.

Located at the end of the Kelvin Peninsula, this walk has excellent views over Lake Wakatipu. Across the lake loom Mt Nicholas and Walter Peak, while just over the waters of the Frankton Arm are the Queenstown Gardens, although Queenstown itself is not visible. While the track skirts the golf course, the course is virtually invisible for most of the walk, which meanders along the shore through schist rock and trees. Later, the track veers to the right alongside the golf course and reaches a gravel road. Walk up this road away from the lake and around the golf course and back to the car park.

Alexandra

19 Poolburn Gorge, Otago Central Rail Trail
Easy 🚶 1¾ hours return

✳ An early twentieth-century viaduct along with two tunnels feature on this flat but spectacular section of the Rail Trail.

➤ From Alexandra, head north to Omakau, and at Omakau turn right into Ida Valley Road. After 10 km turn left into Auripo Road and continue for 12 km to Thurlow Road on the left. The Rail Trail is just a short distance down this road. You can also start from Lauder, which will add another 40 minutes in total to the walk.

Despite early opposition to the idea, the Rail Trail now attracts thousands of visitors to Central Otago to cycle, walk or horse-ride all or part of this 150-km stretch of the old Clyde to Middlemarch railway line. Operating for over 80 years, the line was closed in 1990 and acquired by the Department of Conservation in 1993, eventually to reopen in 2000 as the Otago Central

Rail Trail. The trail is divided into six sections, each between 19 and 32 km in length, and passes through tunnels, over bridges and viaducts, and through some of New Zealand's most dramatic landscape. While biking is a popular mode of travel, this short walk takes in the most scenic part of the trail.

From Thurlow Road, the track follows the flat rail line to the Poolburn Viaduct. This is the highest viaduct on the Rail Trail, rising 37 metres above the gorge. Built in 1904, the viaduct stands on massive beautifully crafted stone piers, the material for which was quarried and shaped on location. Much of the old timber remains, with the spikes that held the rails in place still visible, while some of the old railway iron is stacked on the viaduct's northern side.

Both tunnels are short, so you don't need a torch, but the first one curves slightly so you will need to give your eyes a little time to adjust. Between the two tunnels, the views of the rocky Poolburn Gorge below are spectacular, and a short walk to the top of the longer tunnel affords panoramic views over the surrounding countryside. The gorge is also home to the New Zealand falcon, which can be seen patrolling between the rocky walls for its prey. If you're keen on a picnic, just beyond the exit to the first tunnel you can scramble down the hillside on a rough track to a pleasant shady spot beside the river.

The Rail Trail is very popular with cyclists, some of whom are not particularly considerate to walkers, so take care.

20 Alexandra Clock and the Shaky Bridge

Easy   🚶   50 minutes return

✳ Take in two of Alexandra's most famous landmarks on a good walk from the town.

➤ From the centre of town (SH85), take Tarbert Street and then turn right into Walton Street. After 100 metres turn left into the open area along the river and follow the track to the Shaky Bridge.

Affectionately known as the Shaky Bridge, the Manuherikia River suspension bridge was built in 1879 to handle light traffic, and replaced dangerous river crossings by punt. Superseded by a more substantial bridge in 1906, the older span fell into disrepair, but was finally restored as a footbridge in the early 1950s. Slung between two stone pylons, the bridge does indeed shake and rattle when walked across.

After crossing the bridge, turn left and walk uphill where you will see the track to the clock leading off to the right. The last section right below the clock is a bit steep but not difficult, and you will be rewarded with views over Alexandra and the valley. With a face measuring 11 metres in diameter, the clock was erected by local Jaycees and was officially started at noon on 14 December 1968.

21 Earnscleugh Historic Tailings Easy 🚶 Allow 30 minutes

✳ A 'moonscape' of riverbed stones and rocks left over from the gold-mining era.

➤ Cross over the Clutha River Bridge at Alexandra heading south-west, and turn right into Earnscleugh Road. After 3 km, turn right into Marshall Road and the walk begins down the end.

Hectare after hectare of heaped shingle and stone are all that remain of an industry that boomed along the Clutha River in the early twentieth century. Gold was discovered here in 1862, and once the easily worked ore was exhausted, dredges moved into the riverbed with only varying degrees of success. In 1895 the invention of the tailings elevator enabled dredges to stack the debris behind them, and now they could work into the river bank, rather than just the bed. At its height, 20 dredges plied the river between Alexandra and Clyde, leaving a desolate but fascinating landscape in their wake.

The tailings are part of the Otago 150th Anniversary Walkway that runs from Alexandra to Clyde, but unless you want to walk all that way just wander around the tailings until you've seen enough.

22 Flat Top Hill and Butchers Dam Easy

✳ Excellent information boards make this short walk though dry tussock land worth a visit.

➤ On SH8, 5 km south of Alexandra.

🚶 Loop walk: 30 minutes
To Flat Top Hill summit: 2 hours return

Flat Top Hill lies at the foot of the Old Man Range and is a rare example of short tussock grassland that has its own distinctive natural history, alongside other plants and animal life that have adapted to the fascinating geology of this harsh dry environment.

Gold was first discovered here in 1862, and originally the town was called Hill's Gully, then Londonderry, and then Butchers Gully, a name that finally stuck, though nothing now remains of the settlement. The dam itself was constructed between 1934 and 1937 primarily for irrigating local orchards.

The loop takes around 30 minutes, with excellent interpretive panels along the way. A walk up the slope to the summit of Flat Top Hill is longer than it looks and will take up to 2 hours return; from the top there are great views over Alexandra and the Clutha River.

23 Horseshoe Bend Suspension Bridge Easy

* One of the last surviving historic suspension bridges across the Clutha.

➤ From SH8, cross the river at Millers Flat and follow the road along the river for 7.5 km.

🚶 To the bridge: 20 minutes return

To SH8: 1 hour one-way

Completed in 1913, Horseshoe Bend is one of the few remaining suspension bridges over the swift-flowing Clutha River. Partially constructed from old railway iron, the bridge gave access to the small mining settlement on the eastern side of the river, which has long since disappeared. From the bridge, the track continues through farmland to SH8 and it is worthwhile combining this walk with a visit to the grave of 'Somebody's Darling', which is 1.5 km further down the road.

Central Otago

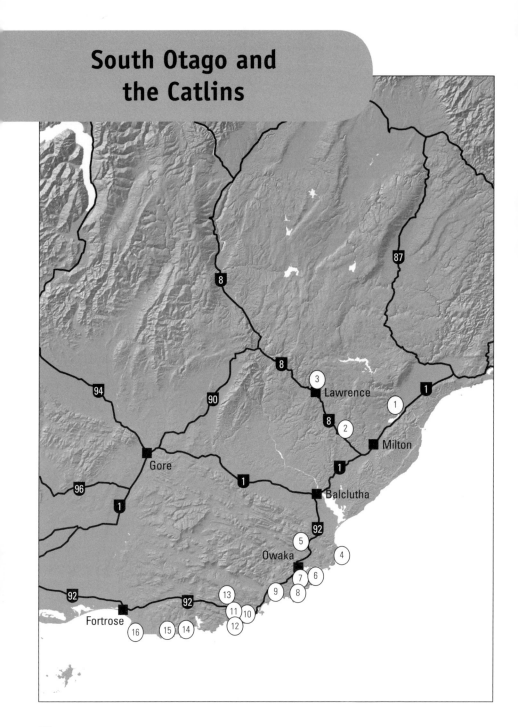

South Otago and the Catlins

1 Sinclair Wetlands   Easy   𝕏   1 hour return

- ✳ Easily accessible, these are the only remaining wetlands on the Taieri Plain.

- ➤ 854 Clarendon–Berwick Road, South Taieri. This road runs west of Lakes Waihola and Waipori and is off SH1 south of Mosgiel.

By their very nature, wetlands are flat and damp, and it is often hard to actually see anything. The Sinclair Wetlands, however, are fortunate in having a causeway through their heart, linking two small islands, both of which have excellent views over the entire reserve.

Covering 315 hectares, and adjoining Lakes Waihola and Waipori, these wetlands are all that remains of the huge swamp that once covered most of the Taieri Plain, and has long since been drained for farmland. Moreover, they have survived only through the far-sighted actions of Horrie (Horace) Sinclair, who purchased the land in 1960 and allowed it to revert to its original state, thereby saving one of the country's most important wetlands. In addition to 40 bird species that breed here, another 45 have been recorded. There is camping and backpacker accommodation on site (ph 03 486 2654) and a koha/donation is requested to enter the wetlands.

2 Manuka Gorge Tunnel   Easy   𝕏   30 minutes return

- ✳ A beautifully constructed rail tunnel complete with glow-worms.

- ➤ On SH8, 11.5 km from the SH1 turn-off, 3 km south of Milton.

The brick-lined Mt Stuart tunnel is 442 metres long and was part of a railway opened in 1876 from Milton to Alexandra linking the coast with the goldfields further inland. The walk is flat and glow-worms can be seen at the wetter, eastern end of the tunnel. A torch is helpful if not essential.

3 Gabriels Gully   Medium   𝕏   1 hour return

- ✳ The first place in New Zealand to experience a gold rush.

- ➤ From the main street of Lawrence (SH8), turn into Gabriels Gully Road and drive a further 4 km to the car park.

South Otago and the Catlins

Lured to the area by rumours of earlier discoveries, Gabriel Read struck gold here in May of 1861, the first major strike in New Zealand. Within months, 6000 miners poured into the area and nearby Lawrence quickly blossomed into a town of over 11,000 people (at a time when Dunedin had a population of around 6000). Gold was also discovered in several locations nearby, but the easy gold was quickly won and the miners then moved on to new discoveries on the West Coast. Later, substantial numbers of Chinese moved in to rework the goldfields, though few made their fortunes, and even fewer returned to China. The small local museum in Lawrence has excellent displays on the gold era including the contribution of the Chinese miners.

Almost nothing tangible now remains at Gabriels Gully – what wasn't carted off to be used elsewhere has long since quietly rotted away in a climate much wetter than further inland. Today the site is overgrown with sycamore, broom, gorse and manuka, but excellent interpretive panels that include historical photos make the walk worthwhile. The loop walk begins with a steady uphill section with an overview of the valley, and then drops into the gully and meanders among old workings, the most substantial of which is a tunnel. A little way on from the car park is a small pond and a picturesque picnic area set among shady trees.

The Catlins

For years the south-eastern corner of the South Island was very much a remote destination, but in recent times it has become one of the more popular driving trips in the country, though fortunately it does not yet attract bus tourist trade. There are good facilities and accommodation at both Balclutha and Owaka, and especially appealing is the fact that most of the short walks are either on or just a short distance off SH92. Most visitors travel north to south, and the walks are ordered in this direction, though the general area known as the Catlins straddles both the South Otago and Southland regions. The southern section of this coast is more correctly known as Chaslands.

The weather in the Catlins can be wild, wet and windy, but this is also part of its special charm. Expect to encounter wildlife on any of the beaches, including blue and yellow-eyed penguins, fur seals, sea lions and sea elephants. Seals often roll in the sand and rest quietly on the beach or in the dunes and can be hard to see. They can also be very aggressive when surprised and move quite fast when disturbed, so keep your distance.

4 Nugget Point   Easy   🚶   30 minutes return

* Amazing coastal views, an historic lighthouse, and wildlife on the rocks below.

➤ From Balclutha, drive to Port Molyneux and then on to Kaka Point and follow the unsealed coast road for 8 km to Nugget Point.

Wild and windswept Nugget Point is named after the group of jagged rocks just offshore, and this track leads out to the most spectacular views both north and south along the coast. The historic lighthouse on the point was built in 1870 when Port Molyneux, just to the north, was an important port and the rugged Catlins coast took a high toll on shipping.

Just before the lighthouse a steep track leads down to Roaring Bay (10 minutes one-way), where there is a hide to watch both the blue and yellow-eyed penguins that come ashore to nest late in the day. On the rocks below the point is a unique seal colony, the only place in New Zealand where elephant seals, fur seals and Hooker's sea lions share the same territory. The seals are hard to see as the track is 130 metres above the rookery, and as these animals easily blend in with the colour of the rocks binoculars are very useful.

5 Tunnel Hill   Easy   🚶   20 minutes return

* A beautifully constructed railway tunnel built in 1895.

➤ 3 km north of Owaka on SH92.

Constructed with pick and shovel, this 276-metre-long rail tunnel on the Catlins branch line was opened in 1895 and closed in 1971, when the timber that was the mainstay of the line began to run out. A torch is useful, especially if you want to admire the fine stonework on the lower half of the tunnel and the brickwork above. For those interested in railway history, an old station and goods shed still stand at Maclennan further to the south.

South Otago and the Catlins

6 Surat and Cannibal Bays   Easy

✳ Two rugged sandy bays noted for their surf and wildlife.

➤ Turn off SH92 at Owaka and drive toward Pounawea. After 2 km turn left over the bridge and continue down this road a further 3 km to the beach access.

🚶 To Surat Bay: 30 minutes return

To Cannibal Bay: 1½ hours return

Surat Bay lies just to the north of the Owaka River and is a wide sandy beach frequented by seals and sea lions. Walk north along the beach and over a low ridge to False Islet and Cannibal Bay. This magnificent sweep of deserted beach is one of the Catlins' best surf locations. The walk can also be done in reverse from Cannibal Bay.

7 Pounawea Scenic Reserve   Easy   🚶   40 minutes return

✳ A particularly fine stand of virgin lowland forest.

➤ Turn off SH92 at Owaka and drive the 5 km to the end of the road at Pounawea. The track is accessed through the camping ground.

This superb short bush walk through virgin forest has all the important lowland trees helpfully identified, including totara, southern rata, rimu, miro and kahikatea. The birdlife is prolific and the song of the bellbirds is a constant accompaniment.

The walk begins in the camping ground straight ahead past the office at the main gate and forms a loop through the bush back to the far side of the ground. A side track leads down to a lookout over the Owaka River estuary. Located in the estuary by the car park is an historic 'dolphin', a simple wooden structure situated in the middle of the river and designed to assist boats turning in the channel's narrow confines. It was built in 1882 at the cost of £25. Very few of these contrivances are still in existence.

8 Jack's Blowhole Easy 🚶 1 hour return

* A booming blowhole located in farmland inland from the sea.

➤ Turn off SH92 at Owaka and drive towards Pounawea. After 2 km turn right into Jacks Bay Road and travel a further 8 km to the end of the road. The track begins at the southern end of the beach.

An easy track across private farmland accessed from the southern end of the beach leads to the dramatic Jack's Blowhole, which you will hear before you encounter it. Over 200 metres from the sea, the hole is 55 metres deep and its boom at high tide is especially impressive. A path runs around the blowhole with two lookouts enabling a good view of the crashing waves below.

From all parts of the track there are excellent views of Jack's Beach, where real Kiwi cribs snuggle into the shore of this beautiful spot dominated by the cliffs of the Catlins Heads. The walk is closed for lambing in September and October and a contribution to the donation box is requested.

9 Purakaunui Falls Easy 🚶 20 minutes return

* Picture-postcard waterfall ensconced in lush beech forest.

➤ Well signposted off SH92 south of Owaka, the falls are 9 km off the main road just past the Catlins River Bridge.

The waterfalls in the Catlins area are not especially high or dramatic, but are more akin to picturesque water features in a bush setting. Purakaunui Falls is one of the most popular such falls in the Catlins, with the water gently cascading down a stepped rock face, and the best view is from the lower lookout accessed by a short flight of steps. The walk is through an especially handsome forest of beech, ferns and mosses.

10 Lake Wilkie Easy 🚶 20 minutes return

* A small lake surrounded by southern rata, which blooms spectacularly in the summer.

➤ On SH92, 5 km south of Papatowai.

South Otago and the Catlins

Fringed by mature podocarp trees, this little lake sits in a hollow below an escarpment, and in summer the rata in flower is particularly impressive. It is only 5 minutes to the lookout over the lake and 5 more to the lake's edge and boardwalk. Keep an eye out for the wily weka along the track.

11 Traill Tractor and Cook's Sawmill Easy 𝄂 20 minutes return

* **✱** Remains of an old sawmilling town and the fascinating Traill Tractor.
* **➤** The track begins on the southern side of the Fleming River Bridge on SH92.

In contrast to the abundant natural beauty of the region, this walk has human history as its focus and in particular the extensive timber-milling industry in the Catlins. The track leads through the former site of the settlement supporting the mill to the remains of the Cook's Sawmill and the restored Traill Tractor. This unusual vehicle is a Fordson tractor adapted to run on rails, either pushing or pulling log-laden carriages from the bush to the mill. At intervals along the track are signs indicating where buildings once stood, though nothing remains today.

12 Cathedral Caves Easy 𝄂 Allow 1 hour

* **✱** A series of spectacular sea caves accessible only at low tide.
* **➤** 2 km south of the Tautuku River on SH92.

This walk is strictly tide dependent and the caves are only accessible for 1½ hours either side of low tide depending on the sea and the sand base. It is a 20-minute walk to the first cave but take some time to explore the other caves along the shore and be prepared to get your feet wet even at low tide. The main cave is over 30 metres high, while others delve deep into the cliff.

There is a small entrance fee and the gate is closed if the tide isn't right. While the tide times are helpfully posted on the gate, avoid disappointment by checking them first at the Owaka information office or on the website (www.cathedralcaves.co.nz).

13 McLean Falls   Easy   🚶 40 minutes return

* ✷ The most impressive waterfall in the Catlins.

* ➤ 1 km south of the Cathedral Caves, turn into Rewcastle Road, and the beginning of the track is 3.3 km on the right.

Not one but four cascades make up the very attractive McLean Falls. The highest single fall is 20 metres high with water spreading across a rock face. The stream is then forced through a narrow gorge for a further three falls. Equally attractive is the walk along the bush stream to the falls, lined with trees and rocks covered with thick mosses, and bellbirds and tomtits keeping you company along the way.

14 Curio Bay   Easy   🚶 Allow 30 minutes

* ✷ An ancient fossilised forest is exposed at low tide.

* ➤ 12 km off SH92 from the Waikawa turn-off.

Fossilised stumps and trunks of trees up to 160 million years old are clearly identifiable on the rocky flat shelf that is Curio Bay. The trees are subtropical in origin, including kauri and cycads, and were felled in a single cataclysmic event, most likely a volcanic eruption. The preserved forest is best seen at low tide.

Curio Bay is also home to a colony of yellow-eyed penguins that pop out of the surf late in the day and shuffle slowly over the rocky ledge to their nests in the flax and shrubs above the bay. Sit quietly and you can get very close to these rare and shy creatures.

15 Slope Point   Easy   🚶 25 minutes return

* ✷ The most southerly point on the South Island mainland.

* ➤ From Tokanui on SH92, turn off towards Haldane and follow the signs to Slope Point, 6 km south of Haldane.

At 46.4 degrees south, Slope Point is the most southerly point of the South Island and is almost equidistant from the South Pole and the Equator. The track crosses farmland that is so windswept even the grass struggles to stand upright, and leads to a simple sign marking the point's position. While it is bleak, there are excellent coastal views across to Stewart Island, and the more northerly Bluff Hill is just visible in the distance. The track is closed for lambing from 1 September to 1 November.

16 Waipapa Point   Easy 🚶 20 minutes return

> ✳ An historic lighthouse and beach and the site of one of New Zealand's worst maritime disasters.

> ➤ From SH92, turn off to Otara, and Waipapa Point is signposted 5 km further south of this tiny settlement.

This attractive beach, often frequented by sea lions, is dominated by the historic lighthouse built in 1884, the last wooden lighthouse to be erected in the country. The light was established in response to New Zealand's worst shipping disaster, which occurred in the early hours of 29 April 1881 when the *Tararua*, sailing from Dunedin to Bluff, struck the Otara Reef just to the north of Waipapa Point. Although the weather was fair, the seas became rough on the incoming tide and several lifeboats were swamped as soon as they were launched. Eventually the ship broke in two, and despite being clearly visible from shore, few survived the pounding surf. Many of the 131 people who perished are buried in the 'Tararua Acre' just to the east of the point.

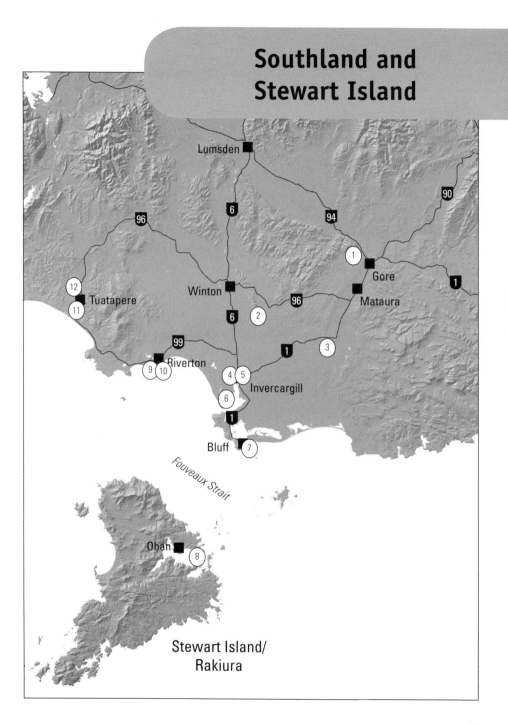

Southland and
Stewart Island

Lumsden

96

90

96

94

1

12

11
Tuatapere

Winton

Gore

96

1

Mataura

1

99

6

2

3

Riverton

9 10

4 5

1

Invercargill

6

1

Bluff 7

Fouveaux Strait

Oban 8

Stewart Island/
Rakiura

1 Dolamore Park and Croydon Bush Reserve   Easy

✳ Nearly 1000 hectares of untouched bush in the famous Hokonui Hills.

➤ Take SH94 west of Gore for 5km and turn left into Kingdon Road. Continue along this road which after 2kms changes into Reaby Road. After a further 5.5km along Reaby Road, turn right into Dolamore Park Road and the entrance to the park is about 1km on the right.

⅄ Loop walk: 40 minutes return

Lookout: 20 minutes return

Dolamore Park and Croydon Bush are two adjacent reserves in the Hokonui Hills and together total nearly 1000 hectares. Never milled, the virgin bush was set aside as a reserve as early as 1895 and is a rare untouched vestige of the forest that at one time covered this area, most of which was felled in the late nineteenth century. The bush is dense and lush, with mosses festooning the trunks of matai, rimu, kahikatea, rata and tree fuchsia.

The Hokonui Hills are famous as the hideout for illegal whisky production during the prohibition era. With the advent of prohibition in 1900, locals set up stills in the deep forested valleys of these hills, and for over 50 years produced the best bush whisky in the land. Whisky from one of the original recipes is now produced legally and for sale at the Hokonui Moonshine Museum in Gore.

The Dolamore Park area has been more formally developed, with an arboretum, rhododendron garden, picnic areas and children's playground, as well as very good camping facilities. Both short walks start opposite the main entrance on the far side of the large grassed area.

The walk to the lookout is on a well-graded uphill path to a point 304 metres high with views south over the plains to Bluff Hill. The loop walk is flat and wanders through mighty mature trees rearing out of lush undergrowth of ferns and moss. For those wanting to stretch their legs even further, the loop walk on the Whisky Falls track will take a little over 2 hours, with Poppelwell's Viewpoint at 460 metres another 30 minutes.

2 Forest Hill and Tussock Creek Reserves

Easy   ⅍   1½ hours return

---

* ✳ A dense island of native bush encompassed by a vast sea of open land.

* ➤ From Invercargill, take the road towards Winton, and after 26 km turn right into Wilsons Crossing Road, then after 7.5 km turn left into Pettigrew Road. The track starts from the Tussock Creek picnic area at the end of this 2 km road.

These two adjoining reserves, just south-east of Winton, contain the only native bush left in Central Southland, and even this was milled for the larger trees. However, this bush contains a surprising number of native birds, a giant rata tree, massive native tree fuchsias, limestone outcrops, small caves and a good lookout point. The contrast between the dense bush, the open farmland of the plains and the stark grass-covered hills could not be greater.

This particular track has the most fantastic gradient, and although a steady uphill, it is hardly noticeable. The 500-year-old rata has toppled on its side, but is still vigorous and growing strongly. From the lookout the views are over the rich Central Southland plains, south to Stewart Island and Bluff, west to the Longwood Range, and north-west to the Takitimu Mountains.

To walk the entire length of both reserves takes around 2 hours one-way and the exit is on Forest Hill Road, 7 km south of Winton.

3 Seaward Downs   Easy   ⅍   30 minutes

---

* ✳ A small reserve with outstanding specimens of rimu, kahikatea, miro, totara and matai.

* ➤ From Invercargill, take SH1 towards Gore, and 2 km beyond Dacre turn right to Morton Mains. Just 1 km past Morton Mains, turn left into Tramway Road West and the reserve is 3 km down this road on the right.

Though Southland has numerous place names that have their origins in the vast forest that once covered this plain – for example Heddon Bush, Ryal Bush, Gummies Bush, Centre Bush – hardly a native tree is left standing on the lowland. This small bush reserve is a reminder of what has vanished and contains not only magnificent rimu but also some fine examples of totara, kahikatea, miro and matai. The short loop walk is flat all the way and, although not signposted, is easy to find and impossible to get lost on. However, take note that it is very muddy in places.

Invercargill and Bluff

4 Thomsons Bush   Easy   🏃   40 minutes

* Pleasant walking through protected kahikatea, matai and beech trees within Invercargill City.

➤ Queens Drive, north Invercargill.

Set aside as a reserve in 1912, Thomsons Bush is named after surveyor-general J.T. Thomson, who planned the settlement of Invercargill in 1857. A surviving remnant of the great forest which once covered the coastal plain where Invercargill now stands, the bush had been milled prior to its protection as a reserve, though today still contains some large kahikatea, matai and beech.

Numerous short tracks weave through the trees, but for a longer walk begin from the second car park (the first is right by the road), cross the small bridge over the stream known as the Waihopai Backwater, and take the first track to the right. This track continues around the outer edge of the reserve, via a section along the stopbank of the Waihopai River and back through the bush to the car park.

5 Queens Park, Invercargill   Easy   🏃   Allow 1 hour

* A magnificent park of immaculate formal gardens and sports fields.

➤ Main entrance is on Gala Street, near the Southland Museum.

The elegant Feldwick Gates (constructed 1913) lead into one of the finest public parks in the country, recognised by the New Zealand Garden Trust as 'A New Zealand Garden of National Significance'. The 81-hectare park is a combination of sports fields and a golf course together with gardens that include formal flowerbeds, a rose garden, Japanese garden, rock and herb gardens, tropical winter gardens, azalea and rhododendron gardens and a bird aviary – in short, something for everyone and all beautifully maintained.

Located within the park is the Southland Museum, with its innovative pyramid shape and famous for its tuatara breeding programme. The museum has very thoughtfully provided an external window onto the tuatara enclosure so that these primitive reptiles can be viewed from the outside at any time of the day, even when the museum is closed.

6 Sandy Point   Easy

❋ Several viewpoints look out over the New River Estuary, Invercargill and Bluff.

➤ From Invercargill, take Stead Street and drive towards Oreti Beach (Otatara). After 7 km turn left into Sandy Point Road and continue down this road for another 6 km. Just past the end of the seal is a parking area on the left.

🚶 Hatch's Hill: 7 minutes return

Noki Kaik Beach: 20 minutes return

Daffodil Bay: 1 hour 10 minutes return

Sandy Point is a large sand peninsula between the Oreti River and the open ocean at Oreti Beach. Much of the area is now highly modified, though patches of bush remain along the estuary. The drive to the walk is like a visual roll call of every conceivable outdoor club imaginable!

From the car park, a short uphill walk leads to Hatch's Hill lookout with views over the wide tidal New River Estuary (which is essentially the estuary for the Oreti River), Invercargill City, and beyond that to Bluff. This prospect is particularly picturesque at sunset. The track then leads downhill to the small sandy Noki Kaik Beach. This area was a rich source of food for early Maori, who maintained small settlements here, and was also for a brief time in 1836 a whaling station.

From the beach, retrace your steps to the Daffodil Bay track, which goes off to the right. This section of the walk leads through a surprisingly dense and dark, but not very tall, forest of matai and totara to another small beach with views over the estuary.

7 Stirling Point

❋ The mostly southerly destination of most travellers around the South Island (though Slope Point to the east is a few degrees further south).

➤ The much photographed Stirling Point signpost points to various cities around the globe and is the beginning of SH1. The point is also the departure point of two excellent short walks.

Foveaux Walkway Lookout   Easy 🚶 1 hour 20 minutes return

This superb coastal walk on an excellent flat track winds around the rocky shore of Bluff Hill through salt-resistant flax and hebes to a lookout point with views both far to the west and to the offshore islands.

Stewart Island, which in one of his rare mistakes explorer James Cook assumed was in fact a peninsula, looms across the choppy waters of Foveaux Strait. American sealer O.F. Smith eventually discovered the strait in 1804, marking it on his chart as Smith's Strait. On his return to Sydney in 1806 he reported his discovery to the Governor of New South Wales. Eventually, however, and no one is quite sure how, the strait became known as Foveaux Strait, after the Australian colony's Lieutenant Governor, Major Joseph Foveaux, who never actually set foot in New Zealand. Just offshore on Dog Island is New Zealand's oldest and tallest lighthouse. At 36 metres, the light was essential to guide shipping through these dangerous waters and first began operating in 1865.

From the Foveaux Walkway a track also leads up to the top of Bluff Hill (265 metres), which will add another 1 hour 20 minutes to the walk.

The Glory Track   Easy   🚶   50 minutes return

This track takes its name from an English ship, the *Glory*, which was wrecked on the rocks below, ironically while taking on board the local pilot. Today the name could equally refer to this glorious stretch of native bush.

The track begins along the coast following the Foveaux Walkway, then loops back through amazing forest. Despite the proximity to constant salt-laden winds and spray, the even temperature and consistent rainfall has created a 'forest scape' that is verdant and lush and contains many fine old trees including kamahi, kahikatea, rimu and rata. The close relationship between the rata and the pohutukawa is abundantly clear, with rata here twisting and spreading much like their northern cousins. In fact, some of the rata are so gnarled and twisted that they look as if they have been wrung out to dry!

From the coast, the Glory Track is a steady uphill on a well-graded path, and not far from the car park the track drops steeply, passing a substantial Second World War gun emplacement and a low concrete lookout pit just below, both built in 1942. This track is very sheltered and a good option if the weather makes the longer Foveaux walk an unpleasant prospect.

Stewart Island/Rakiura

New Zealand's third-largest island is home to the country's newest national park, Rakiura, created in 2002 and covering 85 per cent of the island. The island has an exceptional landscape of untouched bush, hidden bays and rugged mountain ranges, with the highest point Mt Anglem at 980 metres. With just 25 km of road, 250 km of track, and only 400 permanent residents, the island has a gentle relaxed feel (cell phone coverage is minimal), but it does have a good range of accommodation, a great pub and a handful of nice places to eat. The ferry is modern and quick, taking just 1 hour from Bluff to Oban (Halfmoon Bay) – but be warned, the Foveaux Strait has a reputation as a wild stretch of water. The ferry is fairly small and is often booked out, especially in summer, so plan ahead to avoid disappointment.

8 Ulva Island   Easy   🚶   Allow 2 hours

* An unspoiled island is now an important and easily accessible bird sanctuary.

➤ Water taxi from Golden Bay, which is a 20-minute walk from the wharf at Oban.

This island wildlife sanctuary lies in Paterson Inlet, just around the corner from Halfmoon Bay where Oban is situated, and is a popular destination, especially for day trippers. Now that the island has been cleared of pests, rare native birds have gradually been reintroduced and, while as yet not prolific, the bird numbers can only increase with time. Keep an eye out for kaka, kakariki, saddleback and Stewart Island robin. The inquisitive weka is very common too, especially on the beaches, where birds will happily check out your backpack for anything interesting to purloin!

The island is small and relatively flat, with a network of excellent tracks, all well marked and linking a number of very attractive beaches. Sydney Cove is the pick of these and is just a short 20-minute return walk from the wharf, though South West Beach (1½ hours return) is also well worth the stroll. The old post office, over 100 years old, still stands near the wharf.

Should you decide to walk to or from the wharf at Oban back on Stewart Island, there are a number of very short side tracks along the way, including the Raroa Reserve Track and the Fuchsia Walk. In particular, the short hike up to Observation Rock is rewarded with great views over Paterson Inlet and Ulva Island.

Riverton

Riverton began life as a whaling station established by Captain John Howell in 1836 and is one of New Zealand's oldest settlements. Now a picturesque seaside and fishing township on the estuary of the Jacobs River (the confluence of the Aparima and Pourakino rivers), it once promoted itself as the 'Riviera of the South'.

9 Moores Reserve   Easy

✳ Excellent views over coastal Southland and the offshore islands from two commanding lookouts.

➤ Head west from Riverton and turn left towards Riverton Rocks immediately after crossing the bridge over the Jacobs River. After 800 metres, turn right into Richard Street and take the gravel road uphill to the car park at the end.

🚶 Hilltop Lookout: 15 minutes return

Moores Lookout: 45 minutes return

These two walks leave from the same car park and lead to great viewpoints over the coast. Hilltop is a small rocky outcrop that was once used to spot whales passing through the Foveaux Strait when Riverton was a whaling station. The islands of the strait are all clearly visible including Stewart, Codfish, Centre and Pig islands. To the west the prospect extends along the coast to Colac Bay, the Longwood Range, and in the distance the mountains of Fiordland. To the north lie the Takitimu Mountains, Eyre Mountains and the Hokonui Hills, and to the west Riverton, the Jacobs River Estuary, the white sweep of Oreti Beach and beyond that Bluff Hill.

While the views are similar from Moores Lookout, the appeal of this walk lies in the lush regenerating bush with the melodious song of the bellbird following you all the way.

10 Riverton Rocks   Easy   🚶 45 minutes return

✳ A coastal strip of rock and beach with views out to Stewart Island.

➤ Head west from the town and turn left immediately after crossing the Jacobs River bridge, then follow the grandly named Rocks Highway to the very end.

From the car park, cross over the white stile and wend your way along a basic track through lupin and flax over a small rise to the beach. Walk to the rocky point at the far end and return, all the while enjoying uninterrupted outlooks across Foveaux Strait to Stewart Island. Wild and exposed, this attractive walk is great in any weather.

11 Monkey Island · Easy · 𝄠 10 minutes return

✱ Magnificent coastal views of Te Waewae Bay from this tiny beach island.

➤ 1 km south-east of Tuatapere off SH99.

Nothing now remains of this once-thriving port settlement that supplied local settlers and gold miners working the diggings in the nearby Longwood Range. In Maori legend this island, called Te Puka a Takitimu, is the anchor stone of the waka *Takitimu*, which journeyed from Hawaiki and was wrecked at the mouth of the Waiau River.

The origin of the name Monkey Island is uncertain, but the view across the wide expanse of Te Waewae to the Hump Ridge and the Princess Mountains is well worth the short detour. The tiny island is accessible at low tide and a short flight of steps leads up to the viewing platform.

12 Tuatapere Domain · Easy · 𝄠 25 minutes

✱ A thousand-year-old totara is the centrepiece of a pocket of venerable native trees.

➤ From Tuatapere, head west on SH99 and immediately after crossing the Waiau River bridge turn right into the domain. The track begins on the left just before you enter the open sports ground.

Part of the Tuatapere Domain is a small patch of ancient trees that includes totara, matai, kahikatea and beech, the highlight of which is a massive thousand-year-old totara. The walk is flat and easy, and equally impressive is a huge felled tree that was lifted back onto its stump by the power of floodwaters in 1984. The white railing around the oval sports ground harks back to the days when the domain was a horse-racing track.

Southland and Stewart Island

Fiordland National Park

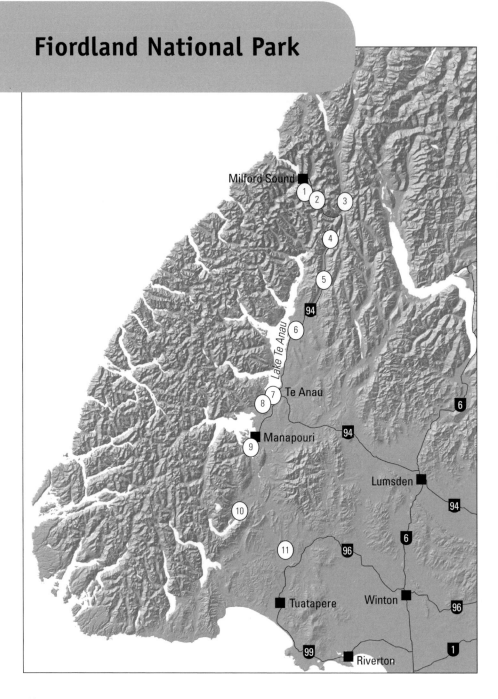

Established in 1952 and with an area of over 1,252,000 hectares, Fiordland is New Zealand's largest national park and in 1984 was recognised as a World Heritage Area. Much of the park is rugged and mountainous with a hard and very wet climate, but this untouched part of New Zealand is spectacular and home to some of the rarest plants and birds in the world. For the average visitor the park is accessible only at the fringes and the only public roads through it are the Milford and Hollyford Roads.

Milford Road

The road from Te Anau to Milford Sound covers some of New Zealand's most spectacular scenery and is the only road to give easy public access through Fiordland National Park. While most visitors tend to travel directly to Milford Sound, take the boat trip and then return, it is worthwhile planning for some short excursions along the way. The road is sealed and in excellent condition, though it is subject to closures during winter, mainly due to snow and ice conditions around the Homer Tunnel. Make sure you have a full tank of fuel before leaving Te Anau, and you will need to carry chains in winter (available for hire in Te Anau), while cell phone coverage is limited to Te Anau and Milford Sound (if that), and facilities and accommodation at Milford Sound itself are very limited.

Bear in mind also that the road is very busy with buses in the morning to catch the midday boat trips; they tend to stop at selected viewpoints on the way to the Sound. Up to 100 coaches per day use the road in the peak of the season, but fortunately most of the traffic is travelling in the same direction. If you want to avoid the worst of the crowds, leave before 8 am and drive straight to Milford Sound, do the boat trip, then stop and do the walks on a leisurely drive back.

The following walks are ordered on the basis of travelling from Milford Sound back to Te Anau and all are clearly signposted from the road.

1 The Chasm   Easy   𝄊   20 minutes return

The Cleddau River is forced through a narrow gorge at this point, creating an impressive torrent of water that over thousands of years has worn the rock into smooth sculpted formations. Given the high rainfall in the area, the Chasm is always dramatic viewing.

2 Homer Tunnel Nature Walk   Easy   ⅄   30 minutes return

Prior to the construction of the Homer Tunnel, the only access to Milford Sound was either on foot via the Milford Track or by sea, and there was considerable pressure placed upon the government to build a tunnel through the Homer Saddle to open up the area to tourism. Government work schemes during the Depression provided a ready source of labour and work commenced on the road in 1929 and on the tunnel in 1935. Progress in the harsh environment was slow and dangerous, and although the breakthrough was achieved, work on the tunnel was halted during the war years. Progress resumed after the war, with the tunnel finally completed in 1953.

The single-lane tunnel is 1.2 km long, slopes steeply down towards the Milford end with a gradient of 1 in 10, and is controlled by traffic lights (though the wait isn't usually too long). The area around the tunnel is 945 metres above sea level and is the highest point on the road, which on the western side is dramatic, with its sheer cliffs and hairpin bends that drop steeply down to Milford Sound. A short walk on its eastern side leads through alpine vegetation and kea are common in the area.

3 Hollyford Valley

✱ If there's time, the Hollyford Valley is an attractive side trip.

➤ Take Hollyford Road, which branches off to the north between the Homer Tunnel and Key Summit. While the road is unsealed, it is flat and in good condition.

Marian Falls   Easy   ⅄   20 minutes return

Not so much a waterfall as a rushing cascade through water-worn rocks in dense beech forest, Marian Falls is viewed from a walkway gantry above the stream that is the outlet for Lake Marian, a small alpine lake above the bush line in the Darran Mountains.

Humboldt Falls   Easy   ⅄   30 minutes return

The total height of these falls is 275 metres, though they descend in three stages of which the tallest single drop is 134 metres. Naturally more impressive after heavy rain, the walk to the falls is through beech forest, though the view of them is quite distant from a lookout across the Humboldt Creek.

4 Cascade Creek/Lake Gunn Nature Walk

Easy   🚶   40 minutes return

A flat loop walk through red beech forest thickly smothered in moss leads to a view of high snowcapped mountains looming over the bush-lined shores of Lake Gunn. The track then follows the shoreline to the lake outlet stream and back to the car park. An added plus is good signage to help with plant identification.

5 Mirror Lakes   Easy   🚶   5 minutes

A boardwalk leads along several flax-fringed tarn lakes that reflect the mountains in their dark depths. This is a popular short stop for bus tours and can be very crowded at times. The best reflections are in the early morning and the late afternoon when the wind has dropped.

6 Lake Mistletoe   Easy   🚶   30 minutes

From the car park, this loop walk begins by dropping down to this small lake ringed by substantial wetlands and with pleasant mountain views in the distance. From the lake, the track follows the outlet downstream to Lake Te Anau. There is a short 400-metre walk along the road back to the start, but be careful as there is no footpath and the cars and buses travel very fast along this stretch of road.

Lake Te Anau

Covering an area of 344 square km and 65 km in length, Te Anau is the largest lake in the South Island and the second largest in the country after Lake Taupo. The east and west sides of the lake could not contrast more. To the west, the rugged Kepler, Murchison and Stuart mountain ranges rise to over 1500 metres and are snow-clad in winter and bush-clad at the shoreline. Three arms of the lake, unimaginatively named South, Middle and North Fiords, reach deep into the mountains, while to the east the landscape is flat, open and much drier. The Murchison Mountains, between the South and Middle Fiords, are the last mainland bastion of the rare takahe. There were only four sightings of the bird between 1800 and 1900, so by the early twentieth century the takahe was thought to be extinct. Then in November 1948 ornithologist Dr Geoffrey Orbell rediscovered the birds in the remote Murchison Mountains, though numbers have since dropped considerably mainly due to predation by stoats.

7 Te Anau Lakeside Walk   Easy   𝄵   50 minutes return

* Views over the lake and observation of rare birds at the Te Anau Wildlife Centre.

➤ Begins from the Department of Conservation information centre on the lake front.

If you're staying in Te Anau overnight this is a very pleasant stroll on a summer's evening or early in the morning. From the Department of Conservation information centre, take the path south along the lake front with views over the lake and mountains until you reach the Te Anau Wildlife Centre. This open park on the lakeside accommodates various aviaries containing native birds, a number of which are not easily seen in the wild and include takahe, weka, kaka, kea, blue duck and kakariki. Some of the birds held here have been injured in the wild or are part of a bird-rearing programme to boost numbers. They are then returned to their natural habitat.

From the Wildlife Centre, head across the road and into the Ivan Wilson Park. This park is a mixture of woodland and more formal gardens and at its centre is tiny Lake Henry, which holds brown and rainbow trout. The park's northern exit takes you back to the lakeside track not far from the start point.

8 Dock Bay   Easy   𝄵   1 hour return

* Pristine beech forest lines the shores of Lake Te Anau on the way to a fetching little beach.

➤ From Te Anau, head south towards Manapouri and turn right into Golf Course Road, then right again at the sign 'Kepler Track' and drive to the car park by the control gates at the end.

From the car park, walk down the sealed road to the control gates and cross over to the other side. This track, which follows the lakeside, is the beginning of the Kepler Track. Along the lake's edge, the track is through virgin beech forest with a lush understorey of moss, crown ferns and beech saplings.

Dock Bay is a very pretty beach of white sand, overhung with beech and kowhai trees and sheltered from the westerly wind, though the lake water is on the cool side even in the middle of summer. If you're feeling fit continue on to Brod Bay, about 1¼ hours return from Dock Bay.

Lake Manapouri

Manapouri is much less developed than Te Anau and at 440 metres is New Zealand's second-deepest lake. However, this body of water emanates a greater air of mystery, dotted as it is with over 34 small islands and containing numerous deep bays and fiords that lead into the heart of the Fiordland mountains.

In 1970 the lake was at the centre of one of New Zealand's greatest conservation battles, the Save Manapouri Campaign – a movement that opposed plans to raise the level of the lake by 30 metres to increase power generation. Over a quarter of a million New Zealanders signed a petition to save the lake and the issue had a significant impact on the 1972 general election which saw a Labour Government swept into office on a platform that included leaving the lake level unchanged.

9 Fraser Beach to Pearl Harbour, Lake Manapouri

Easy   人   30 minutes return

✱ A pretty lakeside walk to the picturesque Pearl Harbour.

➤ Begins by the lake at the junction of the Lumsden/Te Anau roads at Manapouri.

This short walk with views over the lake starts at sandy Fraser Beach and follows the shoreline to the outlet of the lake at Pearl Harbour. This is a great place for an evening stroll to watch the sun go down over the mountains. While the walk can be done either way, parking at the Pearl Harbour end is very limited.

Fiordland National Park

10 Lake Monowai Easy 🚶 30 minutes return

* ✳ A lookout point deep into the mountains with views down both arms of the lake.

* ➤ From SH99, 34 km south of Manapouri, turn into Lake Monowai Road and travel 14 km to the lake at the end of the road. About half this road is gravel.

The Monowai power station was built in 1925 and the lake level was raised to provide sufficient water, yet over 80 years later the result remains evident, with ugly stumps and logs of the drowned forest still visible along the shore. If for no other reason, this lake should be visited as an example of the disastrous and lasting effect on the environment of careless development.

This flat walk is through mature beech forest, the ground thickly carpeted in mosses, and leads to a lookout point that has long views down the two arms of the lake and far into the Fiordland mountains. Camping is available at the car park.

11 Thousand-year-old Totara Easy 🚶 20 minutes return

* ✳ A massive ancient totara in a grove of equally impressive trees.

* ➤ From Clifden on SH99, drive towards Lake Hauroko, and after 5 km turn right into the Lillburn Monowai Road. The trees are 18 km down this gravel no-exit road.

It's a long drive down a gravel road for such a short walk, but the trees here are truly majestic. Worn and weary, the thousand-year-old Hall's totara looks every bit its age. For company, it has a number of other magnificent old trees including other totara, rimu, beech and kahikatea. The trees are thickly hung with mosses, the ground is totally covered in lush crown ferns, and the forest is alive with the sound of the bellbird. The walk forms a loop, and is dead flat and well marked.

Lake Hauroko, which is another 27 km on from the turn-off, is one of the few accessible points in the southern area of the Fiordland National Park, and is New Zealand's deepest lake at 462 metres and one of the 10 deepest lakes in the world.

Glossary

crib	the South Island equivalent of the North Island bach – a small informal holiday home
Jaycee	an organisation for improving the community
kumara pits	storage pits for kumara
moa	any of several extinct species of large flightless bird
pa	stockaded village
pounamu	the Maori name for greenstone or New Zealand jade
taniwha	a mythical creature that inhabits waterways – usually but not always malevolent
tomo	a large vertical hole in limestone country

Other books by Peter Janssen and New Holland Publishers

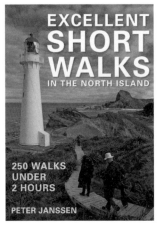

ISBN 978-1-86966-172-4

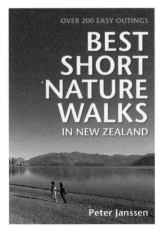

ISBN 978-1-86966-288-2

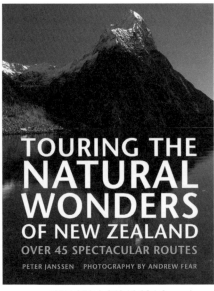

ISBN 978-1-86966-234-9